DARE TO STAND
ALONE

Also by Bradley Booth:
Plagues in the Palace
Prince of Dreams
The Prodigal
Shepherd Warrior
They Call Him the Miracle Man

To order, **call 1-800-765-6955.**

Visit us at **www.AutumnHousePublishing.com** for information
on other Autumn House® products.

DARE TO STAND
ALONE

BRADLEY BOOTH

Autumn
House® Publishing
www.autumnhousepublishing.com
A Division of REVIEW AND HERALD® PUBLISHING
Since 1861

Published by Autumn House® Publishing, a division of Review and Herald® Publishing, Hagerstown, MD 21741-1119

Autumn House® titles may be purchased in bulk for educational, business, fund-raising, or sales promotional use. For information, please e-mail SpecialMarkets@reviewandherald.com.

Autumn House® Publishing publishes biblically based materials for spiritual, physical, and mental growth and Christian discipleship.

The author assumes full responsibility for the accuracy of all facts and quotations as cited in this book.

Bible texts credited to RSV are from the Revised Standard Version of the Bible, copyright © 1946, 1952, 1971, by the Division of Christian Education of the National Council of the Churches of Christ in the U.S.A. Used by permission.

This book was
Edited by JoAlyce Waugh
Copyedited by James Cavil
Designed by Trent Truman
Cover art by Raoul Vitale
Interior designed by Heather Rogers
Typeset: Bembo 11.5/13.5

PRINTED IN U.S.A.

12 11 10 09 08   5 4 3 2 1

Library of Congress Cataloging-in-Publication Data
Booth, Bradley, 1957-   .
  Dare to stand alone / Bradley Booth.
      p. cm.
  1. Gumenuk, Ivan. 2. Seventh-day Adventists—Soviet Union—Biography.
3. Soldiers—Soviet Union—Biography. I. Title.
  BX6193.G86B66 2008
  813'.6—dc22

                              2007049620

  ISBN 978-0-8127-0457-0

DEDICATION

This book is dedicated to Ivan and Vera Gumenyuk,
who were not afraid to be God's witnesses.

It is consecrated to the faithful men and women
in the Soviet Union who stepped out in faith
at a time when the Word of God was being suppressed.
It is a testimony to every Christian in every age
who has dared to stand alone for truth
when all around them men's hearts were failing them
for want of hope.

PRONUNCIATION KEY
FOR RUSSIAN NAMES AND TERMS USED IN THIS BOOK

Andrei *(un-dray)*

Andryi *(on-dry-ee)*

Antonovich *(pronounced as written)*

babushka *(pronounced as written)*

Balkans *(pronounced as written)*

borsch *(borsh)*

da *(pronounced as written)*

dacha *(pronounced as written)*

Dimitri *(dih-mee-tuh-dee)*

feta *(pronounced as written)*

Fastof *(fa-stoff)*

Gumenyuk *(goo-men-uke)*

Hitreshety *(hit-resh-e-tee)*

Kagul *(ku-gool)*

Karas *(kadas)*

Kazakhstan *(ka-zak-stan)*

Kiev *(pronounced as written)*

Kochmar *(pronounced as written)*

Kotovsk *(ko-tufsk)*

Krushenitsky *(kroozj-in-it-ski)*

Larisa *(lah-dee-sah)*

Ludmilla *(lood-mee-lah)*

Mikhail *(mik-ile)*

Moldova *(pronounced as written)*

Moscow *(pronounced as written)*

Mykola *(pronounced as written)*

Natasha *(pronounced as written)*

Nicholai *(nik-o-lie)*

Oleg *(o-lek)*

Petya *(pronounced as written)*

pirogues *(pih-doh-gees)*

politburo *(pa-let-byur-o)*

prianieki *(pree-an-ee-kee)*

Prut *(puh-roodt)*

Pushkin *(pronounced as written)*

Ratovsky *(pronounced as written)*

Sergei *(sare-gay-ee)*

Shevchenko *(pronounced as written)*

Shtab *(sh-tob)*

slava Boeg *(pronounced as written)*

Stefan *(pronounced as written)*

Stravinsky *(pronounced as written)*

Subbota *(soo-bo-tah)*

Tchaikovsky *(chek-ove-skee)*

Tolstoy *(pronounced as written)*

Ukraine *(pronounced as written)*

Viktor *(pronounced as written)*

Vlas *(pronounced as written)*

Yevno *(pronounced as written)*

Yuri *(yoo-dee)*

Zamostyan *(pronounced as written)*

CHAPTER 1

The December morning dawned cold and clear. A thin skiff of snow had dusted the surrounding woodlands during the night, covering the earth with a delicate blanket of white. Skeletons of bare trees stood mute against the rose-tinted sky, and only the gurgling sound of the Prut River broke the stillness of the forest. Chunks of river ice floated in the dark swirling waters, a sure sign that a warm spell had released the sheets of ice upriver. But that didn't mean the water was any less frigid.

Ivan pulled his sheepskin coat tighter around him and tilted his head of black hair to scan the bluff overlooking the river. His intense blue eyes missed nothing and his ears even less. If there were telltale signs of police patrols along the river bottom, he would spot them. The rumors going around said that they would be showing up any morning now.

Ivan was taking a risk meeting here with his church friends, but there was something special about spending time like this out in the raw elements of the winter wilderness. There was a certain sense of exhilaration about it that always left him feeling like he was more of a man.

Meeting secretly like this had become a tradition for the young people in Ivan's church. Most of the ones who attended were boys in their late teens, but there were usually a few girls along too.

Ivan scanned the group. Sergei and Dimitri, two of his best friends, were there, and so were Nicholai, Yuri, and Oleg—and this morning Natasha and Vera had also come along.

There were 15 of them altogether, and a likely band they made. The youth group met for social reasons, of course, but they also met for exercise. Running the paths along the Prut River was a vigorous way to start the day, and it kept them all warm. Sit-ups in the snow and chin-ups on low overhanging branches were exactly what they needed to grow strong and healthy. And when they were too tired to run any farther, a warm crackling fire was always waiting to warm them as they discussed the Bible and what lay ahead for them and their country.

World War II was over. It was 1946, and times were hard. Except for the food a family could grow, there wasn't much to eat. Most of Ivan's friends had fathers who had served in the Soviet army, and many of those fathers had not returned home. Some had been killed in action, and some had been captured by the German war machine and later died in labor camps. Some had come home crippled and despondent.

Being a Christian wasn't easy either. Although Christianity wasn't forbidden in Moldova, it was illegal to have a church building in which members could come and worship. Good Russians were taught instead to follow the teachings of Marx and Lenin. They were to speak only of the Communist Party and do their part to contribute to Soviet prosperity. And of course they were to pay allegiance to Joseph Stalin, premier and feared dictator of the Soviet Union.

Ivan winced at the thought. How could anyone be loyal to a dictator like Stalin? From time to time horrible stories of Stalin's inhuman brutality reached Hitreshety, the small village where Ivan and his friends lived. And Stalin's secret police were everywhere. Stories whispered about the KGB told of family members being threatened and children being confiscated because their parents wouldn't cooperate with the local government officials. And whole villages were sometimes starved into submission.

"The stories are no doubt true," Ivan's grandfather had often told him sadly. "And probably much worse than what is told. Most of what Stalin does is covered up."

It made Ivan sad just to think about it. He longed for better days— right now there was little to look forward to in life. Of course, he and his friends had their early-morning vigils, when they came out to the wooded hollows of the river bottom. It was here that they could step away from the real world for a while and forget their troubles. They could be children again and run and play and laugh. And they could talk openly of God's goodness and His promises.

This is where their beloved church entered the picture. Above and beyond everything that seemed fragile and perilous in life stood the strength of the beliefs that their church had instilled in them. Of course, there was always the chance that this could bring them trouble. The ways of the church seemed to be forever at odds with the teachings of the Soviet state. If Ivan and his friends would only be willing to support the Communist Party and its mottoes, they could be assured of a job and something to eat when it came time for them to take their place in the workforce.

"A job for everyone, and everyone for a job." The Soviet motto seemed appealing, but it always left Ivan with an empty feeling in his soul. Certainly a job could make a boy feel like a man, and those who had jobs could eat. But was that all that mattered?

Ivan rubbed his belly as he thought of the hot drink his mother would have waiting for him when he got home. His mother, Lena, was so kind—always thinking of others. And she was a great cook too. She could make the most wonderful pirogues and borsch. They were the best in the village—everyone said so!

But of course her delicious pirogues could not fix the problems that Ivan and his family faced in their little village of Hitreshety. Only a few hundred common folks lived there, but even in this remote corner of Moldova they knew that they could never escape the far-reaching tentacles of the Soviet government.

Sometimes Ivan wondered if he would ever do anything remarkable outside the confines of his little village. Were there bigger things for him to do for God out there somewhere? He knew that he could serve God in Hitreshety, but he longed to be given the chance to step into a larger arena where he could reach more souls with the precious truths of the Bible. He didn't desire fame and fortune—just that he might do great things for God.

But for now Ivan came to the river every morning, alone or with friends. When it came to spiritual things, being out in nature with God was like a tonic for the soul. Not only was it a perfect way to begin the day—it gave Ivan and his friends a chance to discuss what was really in their hearts. Standing firm for the God of their fathers was what mattered most. It was what they had been taught by their parents, and it was what made the most sense in their cold, hard Soviet world.

But coming to the river was indeed a risk and Ivan knew his parents were worried. All the young people's parents were worried.

"They know what you kids are doing down by the river," Ivan's father, Vladimir, had said to him one day. "The police patrols know that you're studying the Word of God in secret, and they don't like it. They know you go there to pray, and one day they will find you there. They will ride in on their horses and break up the meeting—and they will take note of who has come to the river."

Vladimir's eyes grew moist. "And then they will come to take you away to serve in the army." His voice wavered as he pulled out his handkerchief and blew his nose. "They steal away the best of our young people and force them to serve in a godless army! It's their way of controlling Moldova! It's their way of breaking the spirit and soul of our village!"

Ivan recognized that his father was probably right. He was aware that he and his friends were being watched by the police, but at this point in his life, going to the river still seemed the right thing to do. The young people of his church needed to be active. They needed to draw strength and inspiration from one another and from the early-morning prayer vigils.

One of the favorite pastimes of the Bible study group was talking about the Bible heroes they admired. The prospects seemed limitless. Famous Bible greats filled their conversations—such characters as Enoch, Noah, Abraham, Gideon, David, Esther, and Peter. The young people never ran out of stories to discuss.

Ivan put another log on the dwindling fire and watched the flames leap higher. The early-morning air had a bite to it, making him pull his fur cap down a little lower on his ears.

"I've been thinking about Daniel a lot lately," he said as he stared into the dancing flames. "I've always wished that I could be like him—he's my hero. There he was with his three friends, living in a godless land where no one cared about his beliefs or his God. He and his people were captives, so they felt as if they didn't matter to anyone anymore."

Ivan frowned at thought of the impossible odds facing the four Hebrew boys, but then he smiled again. He knew the story well, and it always inspired him. "I love it that Daniel and his friends stayed true to their families and their country. Nothing could make them be unfaithful to their God! Not the king's food or wine. Not the fiery furnace that got heated seven times hotter. Not the den of hungry lions!" Ivan's grin grew wider as conviction gripped his voice. "I think Daniel was one of the greatest men of all time. He stood for God no matter what! He never gave in!"

Ivan turned his attention back to the crackling fire. He held his hands over its warmth and then glanced around the fire at his circle of friends. They each had their own Bible heroes and had shared their thoughts on the subject countless times before.

He was proud to be friends with these fine young people. He and Sergei and Dimitri had recently conducted Bible studies together in a small town not far away. Five people had given their hearts to Jesus and been baptized.

Andrei was already a youth elder in their church along with Ivan. He and Ivan were the youngest ever to be given that honor. Vlas was a deacon and could sing like a bird. Mikhail knew his Bible better than any of them. Natasha was the daughter of their local pastor—and a Sabbath school teacher for the younger children.

And then there was Vera. Ivan smiled shyly as his eyes rested momentarily on her. Her sweet smile and golden hair always made Ivan's heart skip a beat. She wasn't tall, but she was a bright girl and had a light in her eyes that brought life and happiness to any room she entered.

Ivan admired her more than any of the other girls in his church. She was a spiritual leader among the girls, and she was pretty besides. He had to admit she was one of the reasons he always found it so easy to attend the young people's meetings down at the river.

Ivan poked the fire with a long stick, sending sparks jumping into the air. The early-morning sky was turning orange and yellow now. Nothing stirred in the winter forest except a lone raven flying overhead. It cawed loudly at the young people, as if to tell them that their early-morning vigil was a foolish one.

Suddenly Ivan glanced up at the sound of a snapping branch. There above them on the bluff overlooking the river were two local police riding along on horseback. It appeared as though they hadn't spotted the young people yet, but any moment now they would.

CHAPTER 2

For an instant Ivan froze, wondering what he should do. He held his finger to his lips, but not before one of the girls gasped. Ivan glanced around his circle of friends. Nobody moved—they all seemed rooted to the spot. Ivan had often considered the possibility of a run-in with the police, but now he seemed unable to make a decision. Should they turn themselves in? Should they run and hide?

"Help us, Lord!" his mind raced. "Help us to know what to do!"

In an instant the answer came. It was as if lightning had struck on a clear blue day. Flinging the stick into the fire, Ivan quietly commanded, "Follow my example!"

The young people all turned to him in confusion.

"Do as I do!" he urged. "There's no time to explain!"

He turned and began jogging along the riverbank away from the oncoming horsemen. As the group fell in line behind him, Ivan began chanting, "'Standing by a purpose true, heeding God's command. Honor them the faithful few, all hail to Daniel's band!'"

Ivan glanced over his shoulder at Sergei and Dimitri following close behind. His brow puckered and his eyes practically shouted, "Sing!"

Sergei and Dimitri quickly joined in as Ivan began the chorus, "'Dare to be a Daniel! Dare to stand alone! Dare to have a purpose firm! Dare to make it known!'" Everyone was smiling now—by the end of the chorus they had all chimed in.

At sound of the young people running and singing, the police spurred on their horses and began following them. As they trailed along on the bluff above the river they could see the young people through the weeping willow trees below.

Ivan didn't slow up for a second as he continued chanting. "'Many mighty men are lost, daring not to stand, who for God had been a host by joining Daniel's band!'"

As the young people jogged along, Ivan saw a clearing in the trees ahead and a break in the bluff where the ground sloped down toward the river. Glancing over his shoulder, he noted that the officers on horseback were rapidly gaining on them. Soon the officers would reach the break in the bluff and turn to come down to the riverbank. There it would be much easier for them to identify each individual person. Ivan couldn't allow that to happen—he had to think of something, and quickly.

"Please, Lord!" Ivan looked toward heaven again. "Show me what to do! You're my only hope!"

Again the answer came. Immediately Ivan turned in midstride and jogged toward the river. Everyone turned and followed him as though they were part of some giant centipede. "'Many giants, great and tall, stalking through the land . . .'"

The Moldovan police were descending the bluff toward them now, but the young people had already reached the river's edge. Without a moment's hesitation Ivan ran splashing into the water, followed by the rest of the group as they sang. "'. . . headlong to the earth would fall, if met by Daniel's band!'"

The mouths of the police officers dropped open and they pulled their horses to a stop. "That river's got ice in it!" one of the officers growled. "Are those kids crazy?"

"They must be!" the second officer snorted. "But they'll catch their death of pneumonia for it!"

Now halfway through the river the young people slogged through waist-deep water. "'Hold the gospel banner high, on to victory grand!'" Their voices wavered as they struggled to keep their footing. The rocks on the river bottom were slippery and chunks of river ice floated all around them. "'Satan and his host defy, and shout for Daniel's band!'"

All the officers could do was shake their heads in amazement. At the sight of the young men and women struggling through the icy river, they had completely forgotten what they had come there to do.

The first officer got off his horse and walked down to the river's edge to get a better view of the young people. "Those kids have real backbone!" He muttered as he took off his fur hat. "It's a shame that we don't have more of their type in the military."

"Da! They are the kind the Soviet army needs!" agreed the second officer.

Ivan and his friends were pushing their way up the opposite bank now. "'Dare to be a Daniel! Dare to stand alone! Dare to have a purpose firm! Dare to make it known!'"

The military police had never seen anything like it! It was phenomenal! Even inspirational! How could they stand in opposition to this kind of stamina and dedication, even if it was displayed by a group of young people doing something that was against the law!

As the group jogged up out of the water and down the riverbank on the other side, the officers heard them chanting the words to the chorus over and over: "'Dare to be a Daniel! Dare to stand alone! Dare to have a purpose firm! Dare to make it known!'"

The river water had been frigid, chilling the young people instantly. They were soaked from the waist down, and now the wind rushing down over the bluff made the cold even more numbing. By the time the group had run only a kilometer or so, Ivan could feel his teeth chattering uncontrollably.

Where should they go? Home? The dirt road that ran along the river and on into the village of Hitreshety was the most direct route—about six kilometers—but Ivan was worried that the police might be waiting for them there. Had the police already identified them? If not, they might want to get near enough to have a good look.

To avoid the police altogether, they would probably have to go home another route, and that meant running for a longer distance. But there seemed to be no other way.

In order to avoid the police, Ivan guessed that they would have to run north through the woods, then veer east and south to cut across the fields into town. He figured that route would be about eight kilometers. And even then they would have to ford the river one more time. There were no bridges except on the main roads, and they couldn't take the chance of being seen again so soon.

The group plodded doggedly on over the snowy bluff and into the forest beyond the upper ridge. Stumbling along, shaking from the cold, they crashed through underbrush, tripped over hummocks of swamp sedge, and fell into mudholes covered by patches of thin ice. They had so far to go, and they were so cold—so absolutely, desperately cold!

CHAPTER 3

As Ivan glanced back at the other young people stumbling along behind him, he noticed that their skin was chalky white and their clothes were frozen stiff. He could no longer hear the water squishing in their shoes—it was already frozen.

Ivan began to doubt that he had made a good decision in having the young people march through the river. Had the Holy Spirit indeed impressed him to do such a thing or had it simply been a foolhardy idea of his own? He had been so intent on escaping from the police and eluding the authorities that the idea of crossing the river had seemed a good plan at the time. How could he have been so stupid?

The weather this year had been warmer than most, but unless God intervened, some of the young people might begin suffering from hypothermia. Even worse, frostbite could set in, and then their feet and hands would freeze.

Should they stop and build a fire to get warm? It would take a while for them to get a fire blazing, even if they could find firewood that was dry enough. Ivan had almost decided to do so, but when he felt for the matches in his trousers pockets, he discovered they had gotten wet while he was splashing his way through the river.

He realized that there was nothing left to do but pray and keep running. They would have to trust that God would help them get home in time to keep from freezing.

The distance seemed to stretch on and on to the young people—they were so cold now that their legs felt like sticks of wood as they pounded along mechanically. When they finally came to a shallow stretch of water in the river just outside the village, Ivan plunged in to lead the way. The water felt strangely warm after running in the biting wind, but Ivan knew they didn't dare allow themselves to be fooled by the false sensation.

"Keep running!" he shouted to the stragglers. "Don't stop for anything!"

Ivan winced at the thought of what was going to happen next. He and his friends would probably make it home—but after pulling up close to the warm home fires, the thawing sensation in their limbs would become excruciating. In fact, it would become so painful they would likely scream in agony. Ivan's father had told him of just such an experience he had had when he was a boy.

"Freezing your limbs is no pretty picture," he had warned Ivan. "If it ever happens to you, be sure not to warm up too quickly. Rub snow on your hands and feet so that sensation returns slowly. As it is, you are going to be in terrible pain, but hopefully the damage to your skin and joints won't be permanent."

The young people were now within a kilometer of Hitreshety. As the group floundered up out of the river bottom and into the village, Ivan tried to share his father's warning with the others, but by now they were so disoriented that he doubted that any of them heard him.

In time they did recover, but not without discomfort, and some of them did end up with a touch of frostbite. But they all agreed it was worth the pain and suffering.

"Anything to escape being caught and identified by the police!" Dimitri later laughed.

"And anything to be able to keep up our tradition of meeting in the morning down by the river!" Ivan chimed in.

But the young people had other places they could study as well. Sometimes they met in the inner rooms of their homes. Sometimes in root cellars. When they met at night, the Bible studies had to be conducted in almost complete darkness. One never knew when a police officer might be walking the dark night streets. When the weather was warm, sometimes they would meet on their rooftops on the back side of their homes, or deep in the forest. As a rule they stayed away from the rivers and streams at night, because the police would always be on patrol then, suspicious that the Christians would baptize their new members under cover of darkness.

It wasn't easy to be forced to worship like this, but it was all they had ever known. Some of their parents and grandparents could remember days gone by when there was more religious freedom, but that was before the days of Stalin.

For decades the church had been operating underground, and even under Stalin's oppressive regime, it showed no signs of slowing. The more secret it was, the faster the church seemed to grow. Evangelistic meetings, Bible studies, and even baptisms were conducted in such a way that no one knew who had been at the meetings, and no one knew who was studying the Bible with whom. No one knew how many church members there were in the U.S.S.R., or even in Moldova or the Ukraine, for that matter. No one dared keep records of such things for fear that this information might somehow be discovered. Imprisonment or exile to Siberia awaited those who were exposed.

But in spite of the religious persecution the Christians suffered, few seemed to be really frightened by the police and the KGB. Maybe it was because they were too busy going about their Father's business. Maybe it was because they loved Jesus so much that they didn't care what price they had to pay for practicing their faith. And maybe it was because they knew they had something even the KGB would want, should the agents discover what the Adventist message was all about.

No matter what the reasons, the church did flourish and prosper, and it was the young people who led out more often than not. Most congregations were small ones, meeting in individual homes. Pastors were few and far between, because there was little money to sustain pastors, and it was against the law to be a pastor anyway.

But teachers were permitted, and everyone could be a teacher in his own right. Anyone with the love of God in his heart could be a witness for Jesus and teach from the Bible. Young men were taught from an early age how to be teachers and evangelists for God. Instruction was given in secret though, and even the wives of young church workers didn't usually know where they were being taught.

One night not long after their narrow escape at the river, the young people's church group met to study together at Ivan's home. The topic of army service came up, and several of the boys spoke of their concerns.

"Most of us are old enough to serve now," Sergei said. "Whether the police catch us at the river or not, they're going to come for us one of these days."

"He's right," Ivan agreed. "The question we should be asking ourselves is not how to avoid them. We should be focusing more on what we will do *when* they do call us to serve. What we need to do is pray and study." Ivan could barely make out the silhouettes of the other young people as he peered around him in the inky blackness. "We need to ask God to give us wisdom so that when we get to the army, we can keep the Sabbath in ways that will draw attention to God and His day of rest. And we need to be ready to eat only foods that will honor God, as Daniel did—no pork or catfish, even if they feed it to us on a silver platter."

"Well, don't worry about that," Andrei laughed. "No one's going to serve us anything on a silver platter—a tin plate is more like it."

Everyone joined Andrei, laughing at his jokes, until Dimitri brought up the subject of guns. "What are we going to do if they make us carry a gun?"

"We'll register as medics," Ivan said. "That's what Seventh-day Adventists usually do when they go into the army."

"I know that," countered Dimitri. "But what if they decide they're not going to let us do that? Someday, somewhere, some of us are going to be asked to carry a gun. Not on the battlefield, maybe, but they'll ask us to carry one just the same—first it will be at target practice. And then when we get out into a battle someplace and the bullets are flying thick and fast, they'll push a gun into our hands and say, 'Shoot it! Don't ask questions! Don't protest! Just shoot it!' What will we do then?"

Ivan raised his hands helplessly, but spoke with growing conviction in the darkness. "Well, I can think of only a couple things we can do. We can refuse to carry a gun and take the consequences, or . . . we can be the best medics they've ever seen."

The boys liked that concept—being the best medics in the business. It seemed to ring true to all the other things they had learned about witnessing for God. Just as Daniel and his three Hebrew friends had become the best wise men in all Babylon, Ivan and his friends resolved to become the best medics the Soviet army had ever drafted. They would learn all they could about medicine and how to care for wounds.

But the boys determined to do even more than that. Ivan asked one of the old babushkas in the village to teach the boys about the kinds of herbs that would heal wounds. And he quizzed his mother about the simple home remedies she used when she treated various ailments— such things as hot and cold compresses to help bring the fever out of an invalid, charcoal to cure dysentery in the intestinal tract, and even how to sprout grain to give people fresh greens containing vitamins that were greatly needed during winter.

As Ivan helped train the boys in the arts of healing, he could feel the ominous storm clouds of the unknown brewing on the horizon. Just what lay ahead he couldn't tell, but something within him warned that his days in the little village of Hitreshety were numbered.

CHAPTER 4

Ivan! Come quick!" Fists pounded insistently on the door to Ivan's house. "Open up!"

Ivan yanked the door open to find Sergei wide-eyed and panting. "They—they've taken her away—to the jail," he stuttered between gasps for breath.

"Who's in jail?" Ivan asked. "What are you talking about?"

"They've taken Vera away! She's—in the jail right now! We were in—the village market when the police found her there!"

Ivan stepped out into the quiet street. A fresh layer of snow had fallen the night before, and the early-morning air was still.

He shook his head in confusion. "Slow down, Sergei! Slow down! Vera's in jail? What's this all about?"

"They were asking about our meeting down at the river and she wouldn't tell them anything, so they took her away. Handcuffed her and took her away! You've got to do something!" Sergei spoke fearfully, as though he expected Vera to be locked up for the rest of her life; yet it was obvious he thought there was something Ivan could do about it.

"Come in out of the cold, Sergei." Ivan drew his friend inside, then shut the door. He poured a cup of hot tea for Sergei and sat him down next to the stove to get warm.

"You've got to come to the jail and get her out." Sergei said between sips of the hot drink. "We can't leave her there!"

Ivan stirred the coals in the stove and threw another log onto the glowing embers. "Sergei, did Vera tell you to come and get me?" He stared intently at his friend.

"Well, no." Sergei looked up, unsure of what Ivan might say next. "Actually, I didn't get to talk to her. I just saw them lead her away. She was at the market setting up some cheeses and bread for her mother, and they started asking her questions. She wouldn't answer them, so they just took her away."

Sergei put his cup down. "You've got to talk to them, Ivan—I've seen you do it before! You can say things that none of us could ever get away with!"

Ivan looked at Sergei seriously and then shook his head. "No, Sergei, this time I think we should do nothing. I think it would be foolish for me to go to the jail. This is probably some kind of trap. They want some of us to go down there so they can ask us questions too. Then what will we say? Will we lie? Will we say that we were not down by the river that morning?" He shook his head again. "No, I think it's best if we do nothing."

"But if we do nothing, they'll keep her in jail," Sergei insisted.

"I know, but they won't keep her long. And besides, she's strong. She wouldn't want us to endanger the group." Ivan smiled with a faraway look in his eye. "She may be small in stature, but if she's half the girl I think she is, she'll be fine. Besides, her angels will be there to keep her safe."

Several days later word came that Vera had been released. Ivan went straight to her house, but he wasn't surprised to find her calm and collected. Her face was somber, and he could tell that she was stronger for her experience.

"I told them nothing," she confided. "They asked me over and over about the youth group, but I told them we are not a danger to the Soviet Union. I told them we just like to get together to exercise and talk."

Vera shook her head slowly. "Sergei was there when they cuffed me, and I saw him run off. I knew he was going to get you, and I prayed that you would not come." She smiled thoughtfully. "I knew I'd be all right, and I knew you wouldn't worry about me."

Ivan took her hand. "You're right—I knew you'd be strong. You always have been."

The teakettle began to whistle on the back of the stove, and Vera got up to make Ivan a cup of tea.

"I wasn't afraid in the jail, Ivan, but I am worried that they're going to be stubborn this time around. They're going to come looking for you, too. I can feel it, and it's going to be trouble for all of us. Maybe you should go talk to them. Maybe if you talk to them and explain everything, they won't feel so inclined to think that we're doing something illegal."

"And you think I should be the one to talk to them," Ivan replied, surprised.

Vera sat down and pushed a cup of tea toward Ivan. "If anyone's going to say something to them, it ought to be you, Ivan. You have a way with words, and you always seem to say the right things at all the right times. God has given you a gift."

Ivan glanced at Vera incredulously. "A gift? You think so?"

"I know so! There's no question that you are the leader of our young people's group, and it's for obvious reasons. You were born to be a leader—God has called you for a special purpose, and soon He is going to ask you to do great things for Him."

Ivan wondered at her confidence. Was it because she admired him for other reasons? Had she become enamored with his intense blue eyes or his rugged young face? Did she fancy being his girl? They did enjoy spending time together.

And was he really the born leader she seemed to think he was? Did God have a calling for him? Deep inside Ivan knew she was right, but something else was happening too. A longing began to grow in his heart that this lovely girl would share his life with him. He had long since decided that any girl who would become his wife must first be willing to be a missionary.

And so far she fit the bill—she was already a missionary. Already she had spent time in jail because of her part in the young people's church group.

Ivan wanted a wife who was faithful and devoted, and Vera was fulfilling that dream as well. Her golden curls ringed a face that was truly angelic in purpose—to be true to God first and devoted to him second.

But would she be willing to share his life with him, and would he ever get the courage to ask her? It didn't seem likely on either count, but of course time would tell. They were still very young, and the future seemed so uncertain.

In the meantime there was work to do. If Ivan was going to speak to the police, he wanted to be sure that his spiritual house was in order. He also wanted to be sure that his band of church companions would be as ready to face the consequences as he was. If he were found to be the leader of the church group and then considered a rebellious instigator of sorts, he would probably not fare well. The local police were in cahoots with both the KGB and the military. Just as likely as not, the local authorities would turn him over to one of those two organizations, and right now Ivan wasn't sure which one he preferred. Neither one had a very good track record when it came to being compassionate and humane.

If Ivan should be taken to the KGB for questioning, regardless of his safety, his most valuable possessions must be hidden away somewhere. Like all discerning wives and mothers, Lena would immediately move her son's books, preaching materials, and Bible to a hidden location. Maybe in the root cellar, or out under the hay in the barn, or even behind a stack of wood in the woodpile. This was often done by family members to avoid letting the treasured materials fall into the hands of government officials should they come to ransack the house.

But whether Ivan was taken away or not, he knew his work in the church would go on. The young people's group would continue to prevail—with or without Ivan at the helm. He had no illusions about that. God had worked wonders for the underground church in Moldova as it grew stealthily and yet steadily beneath the infrastructure of Soviet socialism. Not surprisingly, the work of the youth was the backbone of the church's success.

And although Christian meetings were held in secret, the KGB did manage at times to infiltrate the ranks of the church, posing as interested participants. Fortunately the wisest members could spot a KGB officer a mile away. The officers were not good actors.

KGB officials, though present in body, were rarely present in spirit. They appeared unbending, a bit too aloof, always managing somehow to convey that they considered themselves above the common folk. They did not understand the demeanor of the Adventist folks, who freely gave one another hugs of brotherly love. They could not comprehend the character of this bond that gave the church its substance, nor could they match it, and this always gave them away.

Within seconds of their arrival in a church meeting, the leader would temper his statements with kosher comments that would not compromise the nature of the meeting. As a result, the KGB seldom saw anything that resembled a revolutionary spirit against the government, and this always left them baffled. These officers had been schooled in the art of interrogation. Again and again they had practiced the techniques of cross-examination and coercion that would force most dissidents to crack and crumble under pressure.

But the Adventist people were different. They were sometimes obstinate in their unwillingness to comply with government regulations, but only on issues that related to the nature of their worship—such as worshipping on the seventh day of the week. And, of course, they were very tight-lipped about the process of secretly electing their church officers.

However, there was one practice that government officials were determined to search out and eradicate, and that was the publishing and distributing of religious books. The trouble was that no one really knew who was publishing them. Even more baffling, no one knew who was giving them out. Bibles would appear in the most subtle of ways, and when least expected.

At a typical meeting place a new member might look on a shelf or under a chair and find a brown paper bag. Inside the bag would be a Bible with no identification of the publisher, no address, not even a code name to identify the benefactor.

In this way Bibles were distributed so that new members did not have to order or pay for one. This ingenious system was truly a masterpiece of the church's underground work! If new members were asked, they could honestly say, "I don't know who has given me this Bible."

On one occasion Ivan heard a woman, who was obviously a KGB officer, stand up in the worship service and say, "You people are truly amazing! Bibles like this cannot be bought in Russia, and yet here you are in the little country of Moldova with Bibles! No one knows where they were printed, and no one knows whom they got them from! Amazing! Truly amazing!"

The KGB officer left the service shaking her head and never disturbed the company of believers again.

CHAPTER 5

It was a chilly December Sabbath, and the table was set with the best dishes in the house. Ivan sat waiting with his family to say grace. The enticing aroma of his mother's savory borsch and crusty Russian bread filled the small room where everyone was gathered, heads bowed for prayer.

"Thank You, Lord, for every good thing that comes from above," Ivan's father prayed. "Bless our food. We are proud to honor You, Father. May we never be ashamed of You, and may we always be willing to stand for You though the heavens should fall."

Ivan sensed that as long as he lived, that no matter what he might face in the future, he would always cherish these precious days together with his family. The small, quaint house where he had lived all his life held so many warm memories.

Ivan gazed fondly around the small, cozy kitchen with its low ceilings and doorways. His thoughts wandered to the steaming mugs of hot tea or broth his mother made for him in this room on cold winter mornings. In his imagination he could smell the aroma of her warm carrot cake wafting through the house on a crisp fall afternoon, or onions sizzling in a frying pan as she prepared one of her famous dishes.

Closing his eyes, he could almost see the cheerful pink and purple geraniums that bloomed each spring in the wooden flower boxes his mother placed on the windowsills. Out in the yard, a large wooden bucket sat next to the well. The good, sweet water quenched the thirst like nothing else on a hot summer day. Everyone in the village declared that it was the best water around.

Ivan's thoughts turned to the little apple orchard, all snowy white with blossoms in the spring. Later under the August sun those same trees turned dusty green, with ripening red apples peeking through the leaves. But no matter the season, the orchard was Ivan's favorite place to go when he wanted to be alone and think. It was the place where he felt near to God.

A sudden knocking at the door interrupted Ivan's reminiscing and the special Sabbath meal. Instantly his mother and father exchanged worried glances. Ivan had heard his parents talking late the night before, their muffled voices drifting up through the stovepipe hole in the attic room where he slept. Evidently they had heard of the incident at the river with the police. Ivan hadn't told them about it—he didn't want them to worry. But they had found out anyway, and now he could tell they were troubled.

And why shouldn't they be worried? Ivan mused as his mother went to answer the door. It was as if his parents could see the handwriting on the wall. They knew the ways of the government police—both local and military—and the tactics they used to control the local people in the villages of Moldova. These men would stop short of nothing to get what they wanted. Officials like them had all the power in the world—or so it seemed.

Lena returned to the table. "They're here," her voice trembled as she laid her hand on Ivan's shoulder.

"Who's here?" Vladimir raised his eyebrows.

"The army recruiters." Lena sat down heavily and gestured toward the door. "They want to speak with you, Ivan." She put her hands to her face and began to cry.

Ivan closed his eyes momentarily and leaned back in his chair. So the military had finally come for him. The moment that everyone secretly feared had arrived, but Ivan wasn't surprised.

"It's all right, Mother." He stood up and patted her shoulder awkwardly. "I'll be fine."

"But you're so young!" she stammered. "You're only 18!"

Ivan stood silently in the middle of the kitchen, not knowing what else to say. He stared at his father and then turned to his mother again, searching for the right words. "Everything's going to be OK, Mother," he assured her. "I know it will—God has been preparing me for this day all my life. I'm as ready now as I'll ever be."

The army recruiters didn't give him much time to prepare. He was told to report to the town's recruiting office to enlist the next morning. Everything he would need had to fit into an army duffel bag the officers gave him.

And there wasn't much time for goodbyes. Not much time to enjoy the final hours with his family and friends or to savor a few more of his mother's good home-cooked meals. But he managed to squeeze in as much as he could in the few remaining hours.

He and his father spent the afternoon walking and talking in the orchard. It was the best use of the little time Ivan had left at home. Ivan would probably have to enlist as a medic—as had Vladimir. It was one of the few ways he might escape carrying a gun. But even so, Ivan would go through grueling experiences that would test him to the very limits of his endurance.

Vladimir had been a soldier in the Great War—the war to end all wars—and now he talked with Ivan about the difficult times he had been through. Most of the stories he had never spoken of since the war. Even now some of the details were brutally intense and difficult for Ivan to listen to. Ivan had no doubt that these experiences had tested his father's character to the very depths of his soul.

Vladimir told Ivan what it felt like to be in a foxhole waiting for a live grenade or a canister of mustard gas to land beside him. He related the feelings of panic that might sweep over a medic when he had to push broken bones back into the gaping wounds caused by flying shrapnel. He spoke of watching men die screaming and wallowing in their own blood as death rattled deep in their chests.

But not all the troubles were relegated to the battlefield. Vladimir told Ivan about how other soldiers in his unit had made life miserable for him because he was a Christian. They made fun of him because he wouldn't drink with them. Sometimes they even threw boots at him in the dark when he prayed.

And being a Sabbathkeeper had created its own set of problems. The army officers had singled Vladimir out as a dissident, calling him a lazy slacker. They had even sentenced him to time in the military stockade.

But God had helped Vladimir to be strong, and now he assured Ivan that God would do the same for him. "The feelings of peace that can come over a soldier who knows God is His help and strength can't always be explained," Vladimir said solemnly. "Those feelings must be experienced."

Toward evening Ivan helped his mother get some supper ready. He knew she wanted to be brave, but giving up her firstborn son seemed almost more than she could bear. It was heart-wrenching to see her all broken up as she went through the usual motions of preparing the evening meal. She smiled bravely, though, and wiped away the tears with her apron as she made Ivan's favorites food—pirogues.

But saying goodbye to Vera would probably be the most difficult thing of all. Ivan and Vera had known each other since they were children. Together they had attended the little Russian school where the children sat on wooden benches and learned to recite from Tolstoy and Karl Marx. They had gone fishing together in the ponds that surrounded Hitreshety. And they had both been active in the young people's church meetings. A genuine friendship had grown between them long before the spark of love had ignited in their hearts.

Vera came from a good home. She was kind and sensitive and sweet, and at 18 she was already deeply spiritual. Ivan had seen her take on responsibilities in the church that showed she was mature beyond her years. Whenever he thought of marriage, he always thought of her. He believed she would make a perfect wife, but he regretted now that he had never gotten up the courage to discuss such a thing with her.

Ivan wondered how a young man should go about doing that. On the one hand, proposing was such a difficult thing for a boy to do. On the other hand, there was a great fear welling up inside that he would soon be separated from her forever. In fact, the sensation became so strong that several times that day he found himself wanting to run to Vera, get down on one knee, and pop the question immediately.

Yet there was far too much at stake. To do such a thing under these circumstances would be taking quite a risk with both of their hearts. After all, he was leaving quite unexpectedly, and he didn't know when he would return. He barely had time to tell her that he was headed for the army, let alone ask her to marry him.

He would miss her terribly. There was no other way to put it, but Ivan didn't want to think of the great loneliness that would engulf him in just a few hours. He didn't dare. There wasn't time to waste on such things just now.

CHAPTER 6

At sunset the church members gathered to sing and pray in the home of the head elder. By now all the church members knew the sad news. Ivan had to report to the army recruiting office in the morning, and so did Sergei and Dimitri.

After the amber moon had risen, Ivan walked Vera home. She wasn't shocked at the news that Ivan must leave—she had expected something like this to happen sooner or later.

The two of them prayed together as they had never prayed before. When it was finally time to part, Ivan didn't know what to say. He didn't know how to say goodbye to the sweetest part of his life. The moment was almost too painful to bear.

"Just a minute," she whispered as they lingered at the door. "Wait here one minute. I have something for you to take with you." Within seconds she was back, and in her hand was a burnished brass pocket watch with a gold chain on it. It gleamed in the moonlight.

Vera held it out to him. "I want you to have it, Ivan." She smiled in the silvery moonlight, and her voice grew soft. "Whenever you want to know the time, you can check the watch, and then you'll think of me."

Ivan stared at the watch. "It—it's beautiful!" he finally blurted. "Where did you get it?"

"It was my father's. I used to take it out of his pocket every night and polish it until it shone in the firelight. One night when I went to put it back in his pocket, he said I should keep it." She snapped the watch open on its brass hinge. "And look," she added. "It opens and shuts like this so that it stays nice and dry."

"It's beautiful," Ivan repeated gently, "but I could never accept it." He pushed the watch back at Vera. "It was a gift from your father—you keep it."

31

Vera took Ivan's hand in hers and put the watch into it, closing his fingers around the watch and chain. She looked into his eyes again tenderly and kissed his cheek. "Keep it in a safe place, Ivan. It'll be something to help you remember me while you're so far away."

Tears glistened in Vera's eyes. Ivan knew she was trying to be brave, but he couldn't think of anything to say that would help. He was leaving, and nothing could change that.

"I'm not going to forget you, Vera!" He finally blurted. A lump was forming in his throat now, and he fought to keep his own tears back. "I'll think of you every day when I look at the watch, and I'll write you as often as they let me." He took both her hands in his. "And I will come back," he promised. "For you I would go to the Siberian tundra and back if necessary."

Ivan said the words bravely, but if the truth were told, he didn't know when he would be allowed to return home. In fact, given the nature of the circumstances under which he was being called away to the army, he wasn't sure whether he would ever get to come back.

There were more tears and more prayer, and then a promise from Vera that she would walk with him to the train station at dawn.

In the early-morning mist Vera accompanied Ivan, Sergei, and Dimitri to the train station. She had spent many hours with these friends in the church and in their youth meetings. They had enjoyed running and exercising together on the trails along the river, and had often inspired one another with the Bible tales of long ago. But now it was time for them to part.

The train whistled a long mournful call as jets of hot steam shot out onto the tracks from underneath the engine. As the train pulled out of the station, Ivan peered through the fly-specked windows. The last sight he saw in the gathering light of the morning was the form of his sweetheart standing in the train yard waving faintly through the fog.

Would he ever see her again? Would he return to his beloved home and town? Would he worship again with fellow believers?

What about the young people's meetings? Who would lead out? Ivan had been a youth leader for years, but now he guessed that someone else would step up from the ranks and assume the responsibility.

As the train gathered speed and the landscape began to pass by more quickly, Ivan bowed his head in prayer. What did God have in store for him? What hardships would he face? Would there be persecutions for his faith?

A sudden wave of homesickness washed over Ivan as he contemplated the unknown, but he swallowed hard and forced himself to ignore the flood of emotions. Right then and there he resolved to be strong for God and to be brave. He would be true to his faith and all that his parents had taught him.

But he wouldn't stop there. Ivan recognized that there was more to being a witness than just being true to God's Word. If the Holy Spirit was truly in his heart, he would be compelled to tell others the good news of salvation—Jesus had died to save humanity, had risen from the dead, and was coming again to take His people home. That was the good news of the gospel, and it required everyone who claimed to be followers of Jesus to go everywhere and spread that news. Jesus Himself had said so.

As the scenery sped past the train windows, a familiar text from the book of Acts crossed Ivan's mind. He had memorized the words long ago, and now they came back to him clearly as though sent directly from God.

"But you shall receive power when the Holy Spirit has come upon you; and you shall be my witnesses in Jerusalem and in all Judea and Samaria and to the ends of the earth" (Acts 1:8, RSV).

The words rang true like a bell at sunrise. Suddenly Ivan realized that God's plan for him had become crystal clear.

God was calling him to a very special task, and Ivan grew excited at the new revelation. Previously he had thought that the forced enlistment in the army was a roadblock in his life. He had supposed that Satan and his evil forces were thwarting God's plan for his life and keeping him from doing what he loved doing most—being a missionary to the young people of his church and village.

But God's plan was grander than he could have ever imagined.

Ivan stared across the aisle of the train car at Sergei and Dimitri. Was it possible that God had something bigger for the three of them to do, something far greater and wider in scope than running the young people's meetings at Hitreshety? Was God calling Ivan to be a witness for Him in the Soviet military, to bring the good news of the gospel to an army of men who claimed no allegiance to anyone or anything but

the Soviet Union? Was it God's plan that Ivan be a missionary in perhaps the most difficult evangelistic field on earth?

Ivan felt a bit lightheaded as the thought of such a possibility raced
through his mind. The pieces of the puzzle were coming together now.
In some ways he would be like the Waldensian missionaries he had so
often read about.

The Waldenses, a group of faithful Christians during the Middle
Ages, would come down from their homes in the Swiss Alps to share
the gospel with the people in the valleys. But at that time, teaching
from Scripture was forbidden by government and church leaders alike.
Thus it was necessary for the Waldenses to disguise themselves as mer-
chants and tradesmen so that they could come into contact with hungry souls—aristocrats and common folk alike. Whenever the Waldenses
detected a sincere heart searching for hope and spiritual truth, they
shared the hidden passages of Scripture they always carried.

Ivan frowned slightly. Was this what the Lord expected of him?
Was he going to have to smuggle truth into the army camp like some
kind of contraband? Ivan didn't like sneaking around. He much preferred to speak boldly, presenting the truth plainly and simply, allowing
the message to cut like a two-edged sword if necessary.

Closing his eyes, Ivan leaned back in his seat. The train ride would
last throughout the day and most of the night before ending early the
next morning at the army base in Fastof. He needed to sleep, but he
needed to pray, too.

"Please, Lord. Show me what You want me to do. Open my ears
so that I can listen to Your voice. Open my eyes so that I will see opportunities to speak for You. Open my heart so that I will be willing to
be a missionary for You."

A missionary man. That was his next assignment from God—to be
a missionary for Jesus in the army. It wouldn't be easy, but it would be
worth all the energy he could muster. There was no room for doubt.
Wherever and whenever God would lead, Ivan knew he must go.

CHAPTER 7

The sun wasn't even a glimmer on the eastern horizon when Ivan heard the bellowing voice of the sergeant. It took him a moment to get his bearings, but then he remembered where he was. As he pulled his head out from under the blanket, reality hit him squarely in the face—he was in the army.

"Comrades! On your feet! This is no way to begin your first day in the army!"

Ivan sailed out of bed, banging his head on the bunk bed above him. He staggered in the darkness and then caught his balance as the sergeant yelled, "Last man out of the barracks will be assigned to latrine duty for the rest of the day!"

Ivan scrambled to get into the clothes he had been wearing the night before, but then noticed others around him hurriedly putting on their army uniforms. In an instant he shed his dungarees, jumped into his regulation trousers and shoes, and grabbed his shirt on his way out the door. Luckily he fell into line outside just before the final soldier came stumbling out through the barracks door.

The unlucky soldier realized he was the last one out and would now pay a price for it. He hung his head dejectedly as he walked to his place in line.

"Thank you, comrade Yevno!" the sergeant sneered as he stood waiting for the men to quiet down. "It's good to have a man volunteer for latrine duty so early in the week!"

The officer paused and then began to pace up and down the line of bleary-eyed soldiers. "Comrades!" he shouted. "This is your first day in boot camp—the army of the Soviet Union welcomes you! We are here to help you learn to obey the orders of your superiors, and we are here to help you do it gladly!"

35

He spoke condescendingly, as though the men were children. "Don't be afraid! We are here to make real men out of you, and when we are finished, you will be more than men! You will be soldiers!"

The sergeant surveyed the line of men. A hardened look stitched itself across the features of his face, and Ivan couldn't help noticing a nervous twitch in the man's left eye.

"Your time belongs to me now!" the sergeant added, as though enjoying every minute of his tirade. "From now on I will be your family! I will be your mama and your papa. I will be your brother and the closest thing you have to a friend! I will be your shadow! When you think that you cannot stand to see my face another day, I will be there with you like a bad habit!"

He held up a wooden bucket. "And now, first things first, boys! If you have a timepiece, you must surrender it to me!" He held the bucket higher. "Watches and timepieces go in here! Hurry up now! You won't need them from now on—you'll be living on army time!" The sergeant laughed raucously, and his eye began to twitch again violently.

Ivan shot a sideways glance at the other recruits around him. With a sickening feeling he slowly pulled Vera's watch from his front shirt pocket and opened the brass lid one last time. He stared fondly at the gold face, trying desperately to remember its every feature. He hated to lose the watch, but what else could he do? Swallowing hard, he handed it over. It was the only thing he had with him from Vera. He sighed as the sergeant dropped the watch into the wooden bucket. Why had he even brought it with him? He should have left it in the trunk at the foot of his bed. Better yet, he should have left it with Vera!

Most of the boys in his platoon did not own a watch, but there were a few in the bottom of the wooden bucket when it passed Ivan. The sight of those forlorn watches made Ivan feel desperate. He would probably never see Vera's watch again. Some officer or supply sergeant would likely pawn it off for a few rubles in a village jewelry shop somewhere.

The sergeant paused in front of Ivan and leaned into the boy's face. "You boys are going to experience a life of discipline!" he barked, drops of spit flying from his mouth as he spoke. "You will know what it means to go without food! You will go without water and without sleep!" The spit hit Ivan in the eye, but he looked straight forward, not daring to make a sound or even flinch.

"Your lives will be changed forever!" His voice rose to a crescendo. "This is a man's army, and you boys will learn to fight! You will learn to stand together as one!" he roared. "You will learn how to become killing machines!"

Although the morning air was biting cold, it was the officer's words that sent shivers up and down Ivan's spine.

Fight? Kill? Ivan wished with all his heart that he could talk with Sergei and Dimitri to find support, but they had been assigned to platoons in other barracks. All the early-morning talks at the river hadn't really prepared him for the feelings he was experiencing now. Ivan had often thought about what he would do if he were faced with death, but he had given less thought to what he would do if he were forced to kill! Though he and his friends had talked about it, he knew he had signed up to serve as a medic, not a killing machine!

It didn't matter! Ivan knew he could never fight—he could never carry a gun and kill another man. He wasn't cut out for that sort of thing!

Apparently some men could kill and not think much of it. Ivan had seen schoolmates kill birds or small animals for the fun of it, but he had never been able to do that.

Ivan had been born and raised for one thing—to be a missionary! He had been born to share the gospel story wherever God should ask him to go. It didn't matter whether it was at school when he was just a boy, or at the river bottom at sunrise with the youth group, or in the Soviet army now. Ivan could be only a missionary for God. He was not a killer! He was a missionary! There was nothing else for him to do. It was his destiny.

That first day in the army was the most grueling day of Ivan's life. He was glad that he was in such good condition from running every morning with the other young men and women in the church youth group. Here in the army he could easily keep up with most of the other recruits, even staying ahead of them much of the time. He didn't want to think about what would have happened if he hadn't been in good shape. There were many young men that day who suffered at the hand of the platoon sergeant for being too slow or not strong enough.

From sunup to sundown the young men were put through test after test. The sergeants ran them through obstacle courses. They made them do push-ups. The men were forced to do sit-ups and pull-ups until they thought they would drop. And when that was over, they sent them on a 20-mile run over steep hills and through icy swamps—with fully loaded packs. There wasn't much snow on the ground, even though it was already the middle of December. Even so, by the end of the march the recruits were cold and wet, and some even suffered from hypothermia.

Ivan could hardly remove his frozen boots as he sank exhausted into bed. The recruits had eaten nothing all day—not even a scrap of bread. But food didn't matter much to Ivan at this point. All he wanted to do now was sleep and rest his aching muscles.

But if Ivan thought he was going to get some rest, he was in for a rude awakening—literally. After what seemed only a few minutes the sergeant stomped into the barracks again.

Ivan tried to pry his weary eyelids open, but they refused to budge. Somehow he managed to stumble into his boots and out into the bone-chilling wind on the military commons. It was well before dawn, but it didn't seem to matter to the sergeant. The whole ordeal seemed like a dreadful nightmare and the sergeant a horrible monster in it! Ivan instinctively reached for his watch to see what time it was, then remembered that it had been taken from him the day before.

Since arriving in camp, the boys still had had nothing to eat, and Ivan began to wonder just how much more they could endure. His father had warned him that boot camp would be cruel—like nothing he had ever gone through before. Ivan had not doubted his father, but the experience was even worse than he had imagined.

The sergeants ran the recruits through the same drills as the day before. As the day dragged on, Ivan began to understand what it was the leaders were doing. They were attempting to break the men down—to get them to submit to the army's regimen—and the sooner the better. This required the men to give up their sense of identity and to submit their wills to a higher authority.

The strain of physical exhaustion was taking its toll on the recruits, but Ivan knew the mental ordeal would be even more strenuous. Before long, as a Seventh-day Adventist, he was going to have to face even more rigorous ordeals. His beliefs regarding the Sabbath would bring him trouble for sure, and maybe his diet as well. These trials were going to force him to decide between right and wrong, and he needed to have his conscience armed and ready.

But Ivan also understood that when the recruits were finished with basic training, they would be able to perform together as a coordinated, efficient, and cohesive unit. He wanted to have that—if he could manage to last under the pressure.

However, as the drills continued, recruits began falling away right and left. Some were growing angry and belligerent at the treatment they were receiving from the sergeants. Others just didn't have enough energy to go on and collapsed.

Ivan plodded doggedly on, trying to keep an even pace and to catch his breath against the cold wind whipping across the field. "Please, Lord!" he pleaded as he climbed over one obstacle after another. "Help me to do my best and finish this day standing on my own two feet!"

CHAPTER 8

That night the men were finally allowed to eat, but it wasn't much. Just some boiled stew made from onions, potatoes, and cabbage. Many of the men could hardly hold their heads up to eat the small portion they were given, but nothing had ever tasted better to Ivan.

The next morning the men were allowed to sleep in late. The rising shout of the sergeant woke them at 6:00, and to his amazement, Ivan felt like a new man. With a grateful heart he breathed a sigh of relief in thanks to God for keeping him strong.

However, he realized that if he wanted to have any devotional time with God, he was going to have to learn to get up earlier than the other men. He would also have to find a way to keep secret the small Bible that he kept tucked away in the trunk at the foot of his bed. Prayer itself would be no problem. In the darkness of the predawn hours there would be plenty of solitude to pray.

Surprisingly enough, no one bothered Ivan much. He had thought that a Christian in a fighting man's army would be teased and bullied and even abused for his faith, but as of yet that hadn't happened. Was it because God was keeping His protective hand on him? Was it because Ivan hadn't made his prayer life and devotions noticeable yet? Or was it because the other men were just too weary even to notice that Ivan existed?

On the evening of his third full day in boot camp Ivan took some paper out of the trunk at the foot of his bed and began to write letters. His parents needed to know that he was well, that his spirits were up, and that he was adjusting to life in the military. He had promised to write, but until now he had had neither the time nor the strength to jot down even a note.

He wanted to tell them bits of news that would be interesting, but not too detailed—heartfelt, but not too emotional.

And of course there was Vera. She would be worried, and he didn't want to keep her waiting too long. He was careful to write only cheerful comments, nothing that would seem depressing or appear to be complaining. He knew that his superiors would probably screen and censor the letters. Ivan chuckled to himself and then sighed as he penciled the "love letters." The thought of such an intrusion on his private life would no doubt keep him from writing anything that even resembled romance.

But as the week progressed there were other things on Ivan's mind that caused additional worry. Already it was Wednesday, and the Sabbath was fast approaching. As of yet Ivan hadn't formulated a plan about what he would do or say to the officers in his platoon about his convictions. Would they make him work? Would he be thrown into the military stockade if he refused? Would they try to break him? Ivan knew there was going to be trouble, but there was probably nothing he could do about it. He must keep the Sabbath!

The very next evening trouble did indeed find him. Ivan sat eating in the mess hall where all the recruits ate their meals. One of the young soldiers who seemed to have a chip on his shoulder toward everyone in general came and sat down across the table from Ivan. He was a big man with a crew cut, wide shoulders, and big gnarled hands. He was tough and, like Ivan, had been able to take everything the sergeants could dish out. However, his face was hardened and cold, and all the men were afraid to go near him.

As the big man sat down on the bench, he glanced at Ivan and noticed that Ivan wasn't eating the small slab of pork on his tin plate. "What's the matter, soldier boy?" he demanded. "Are you sick?"

"No." Ivan tried to think of something else to say.

The soldier continued staring at him between bites of his own food. "So what's the problem?"

Ivan wondered what he should tell the soldier. That he didn't like pork? That pork was forbidden in the Bible? No matter how he said it, the soldier would think of him as a weakling, something less than a man. Real men ate meat—and the redder the meat, the better.

"I don't eat this kind of meat," Ivan finally said, then braced himself for the soldier's reaction.

Now he had really done it! His answer made him sound finicky, and that was worse than being a mama's boy.

Ivan glanced at the meat on his plate. The rest of his food was almost gone, and he wished that the pork were somewhere else right now, too—in the slop pail by the door, or under the table for the cats to eat, or maybe even on someone else's plate.

But it wasn't. It just sat there all forlorn in the middle of Ivan's plate.

Ivan was tired and just wanted to eat in peace. It had been another cold, hard day out on the basic training fields. He didn't particularly want to give a lesson on health, and he didn't want to make the big man any grouchier than he already was.

By now Ivan half-wished that he had just eaten the meat to avoid the trouble! It would have been a lot easier to eat it than to have to try to explain why he hadn't eaten it.

Since army meat was of very low quality, Ivan was worried the pork would be full of trichinosis worms. But even if it had been beef or chicken, he wasn't sure he would have trusted it. Meat in the army sometimes spoiled or caused food poisoning from not being preserved or refrigerated properly. Someone was always getting sick in Ivan's barracks. Because of this, Ivan had decided to become a vegetarian while he was in the army.

Ivan wasn't really getting enough protein, but for the time being he seemed to be none the worse for it. The occasional servings of beans, lentils, or eggs seemed to give him what he needed.

Ivan looked at the young soldier across from him. He had to say something. Maybe this was one of God's opportunities for him to be a witness in the army.

Without further thought Ivan reached his hand across the table to introduce himself. "My name is Ivan," he said. The young soldier slowly took Ivan's hand, as though not knowing what else to do.

"I don't eat the meat they serve here," Ivan added quickly, and then lowered his voice. "I've heard that it's not very healthy to eat—who can trust it, with all the sickness going around?"

Ivan held his breath. He looked the soldier straight in the eye and waited. His explanation was only a partial one, but what else could he do? He didn't think the big man was going to give him a chance to deliver a lecture on what kinds of foods were forbidden in the Bible. Most likely he didn't even know what a Bible was.

The soldier just stared back at Ivan, his mouth hanging open. His steel-gray eyes met Ivan's blue ones with an incredulous look—almost as though he wanted to hear more. Ivan was sure the soldier had never thought about the meat being unhealthy, but he was also very sure that God wanted him to make an impact on the life of this soldier.

Please, Lord, Ivan prayed silently, *show me what You want me to do. Give me the words I need to reach out to this man and introduce him to You.*

The hard lines on the young soldier's face softened a bit. "You got that right," he finally replied, as he looked at his plate and pushed his slice of pork back and forth with his fork. "It makes sense, but I can't imagine how you survive without eating the stuff. I've been here less than two weeks, and I'm told we won't get meat like this very often." He spread his arms wide, as if to take in the entire mess hall. "I mean, how do you get enough energy around this place to do all the work-outs and drills they require of us? Not by eating beets and cabbage!"

Ivan chuckled at the soldier's attempt at humor. "Well, of course there's bread, too," he grinned.

"That's true." The soldier grinned back and seemed to relax. "My name's Petya. We should talk some more. You can tell me about these strange ideas of yours." Petya winked good-naturedly and then turned his attention back to his supper.

Ivan smiled to himself—so he was strange, was he? He would have laughed right out loud if the moment hadn't been so perfect. Here he was receiving yet another opportunity to witness for God, and things had turned out better than he could have possibly hoped for.

"Thank You, Lord," Ivan mumbled as he left the mess hall. "Thanks for being with me here tonight and giving me the right words to say." A Bible text that he had repeated many times on those early-morning prayer vigils with his friends by the riverside came to mind.

Do not worry beforehand about what to say. Just say whatever is given you at the time, for it is not you speaking, but the Holy Spirit (see Luke 12:11, 12).

CHAPTER 9

He wasn't quite sure what it was, but something woke Ivan in the wee hours of the early morning. It wasn't the sergeant—the sky was still dark, and not a soul was up yet. Maybe it was the horrendous snoring that filled the barracks every night. Maybe it was the barking of the dogs that lurked around the mess hall kitchens looking for garbage scraps. Or maybe it was the wind moaning outside, rattling the windows as it rushed between the rows of barracks.

Then Ivan remembered what day it was. It was Sabbath.

There was no need to pry his eyes open to clear the cobwebs of sleep from his mind. He was already wide awake, and now he knew why. God must have awakened him.

The tall, lanky boy sat up, swinging his feet over the side of the bed. It was time to pray—time to pray as he had never prayed before.

The wooden floor was hard and drafty, but Ivan was used to it by now. He was making it a habit to start every day on his knees. It was the only place he knew to get the answers he would need for the coming day. It was the best place to accept God's will as his own—and today more than ever before.

Time seemed to stand still whenever Ivan poured out his heart to God. As he knelt there in the darkness, memorized passages of Scripture came to mind. "Seek the Lord while he may be found, call ye upon him while he is near" (Isa. 53:6). "Evening, and morning, and at noon, will I pray, . . . and he shall hear my voice" (Ps. 55:17). "[The Lord's] compassions fail not. They are new every morning: great is [His] faithfulness" (Lam. 3:22, 23). "As for me, I will behold thy face in righteousness: I shall be satisfied, when I awake, with thy likeness" (Ps. 17:15).

A feeling of peace seemed to hover over Ivan when he communed with God like this, and he sensed that the Holy Spirit had come to give him strength and courage for the day. It was as though a small part of heaven was there with him in the cold, dark barracks in the middle of Moldova, as though God were telling him that this Sabbath was going to be like no other day in his life.

Ivan finally felt prepared for the worst. If the Sabbath was going to come between him and his superior officers—and he knew it would—then he must face the problem squarely. Whether or not he would survive as a Seventh-day Adventist Christian in the Soviet army would be determined in the next few hours.

The sun had not yet broken the eastern horizon when Ivan stepped out of the mess hall three hours later—he had hurried through breakfast. Shades of magenta, pink, and peach were painting the dawn, and high above in the deep-blue stratosphere hung wispy cirrus clouds. It was cold out, but the day promised to be clear and bright. An inch or two of snow had fallen the night before, so the military commons was now blanketed clean and white.

Ivan bowed his head in prayer one last time as he boldly strode to the main field of the military commons, where all the recruits assembled every morning for basic drill, roll call, and the scheduling for the day. He had given little thought as to how exactly he would pull the whole thing off, or even what he would say. He had been afraid to plan too far in advance, lest his wisdom should get in the way of God's plan. But he had to step out in faith.

He chose a spot near the commissary and then scanned the area for something to stand on. He found what he was looking for when he spotted a large wooden cabbage crate by the back door of the mess hall kitchen. He dragged the crate to the front wall of the commissary, turned the crate over, and stepped up on it to survey the army commons. Soldiers were already assembling for roll call.

This much Ivan knew: right now, in this public place, he was going to make a statement declaring his beliefs as a Christian. He felt impressed that this would be the best way to let his superiors know about his status as a Christian and a Sabbathkeeper.

But Ivan had other reasons for such a bold move. It was very likely that none of the hundreds of other young recruits on the army base had ever heard the name of Jesus before. In one fell swoop Ivan would be able to tell them the gospel story and about Jesus' soon coming.

And now it was time. He needed to get on with it.

Gathering up what courage he could muster, Ivan raised his voice and announced in clear, trumpetlike tones, "Today is the Sabbath of the Lord our God."

A group of passing soldiers stopped and looked at him. "Men, did you know that Jesus Christ is the Son of God? He created this world in six days and then rested on the seventh day. But man rebelled against God and chose to sin against heaven, and our world has been a place of sorrow and sickness and death ever since."

More soldiers stopped to listen. The crowd began to grow in size, so Ivan spoke a little louder. "Now, God loved us so much that He decided to send His Son, Jesus, to live as a man among men. This same Jesus went about doing good and healing men of all their diseases. Thousands of people flocked to hear Him and see his miracles." Ivan paused for effect. "But vengeful men hated Him for His popularity and turned against Him. They arrested Him, beat Him, and turned Him over to the enemy so that He could be executed on a cruel cross."

A murmur rippled throughout the crowd as several sergeants arrived, but Ivan was on a roll and knew he couldn't stop now. He probably had just one shot to do this thing right. Somehow he must include the whole gospel plan in this one speech. There wasn't time to schedule a whole series of evangelistic meetings for the soldiers to attend nightly.

A large crowd had gathered by now. In fact, it seemed that with every passing minute, hundreds more soldiers were arriving. Ivan didn't know how many were present, but he knew that there were about 3,000 soldiers on the military base. The meeting was causing such a stir that many were hurrying over to see what all the fuss was about. When they arrived, however, they found that it was only one man speaking, and he was not a general, or colonel, or even a sergeant. The speaker was one of them, a lowly private.

Ivan kept on talking. "Now, this man called Jesus rose from the dead and went to heaven. Today He is preparing a home there for all who wish to accept Him as their Savior and receive His forgiveness for their lives of sin."

Suddenly Ivan noticed a jeep approaching from the officers' quarters. It was coming so fast that snow was shooting out from its back wheels like bullets from a machine gun. Within seconds the jeep pulled up at the back of the crowd—the driver got out, but an army officer remained seated in it.

Ivan had gone beyond the point of no return now. He would probably be severely punished for disorderly conduct and for causing a commotion on the military commons. He would probably have to spend several days, or even weeks, in solitary confinement in the military stockade. There would probably be a military hearing, and maybe a trial.

But somehow none of that seemed to matter right now. A sense of peace flooded over Ivan, and he knew he must finish his speech.

"One day soon Jesus is coming to earth again to take us home to heaven with Him." Ivan gave the crowd of soldiers a broad smile. "In that beautiful place we will never have any more pain, or sadness, or tears. We will build houses and plant gardens. We will be happy and contented, and we will live for ever and ever with Jesus, our Lord and King."

Ivan was close enough to see that the military officer in the jeep was a high-ranking colonel—the bars and stripes on his shoulders and chest were enough to make any soldier quiver. Ivan knew he should be afraid of what was coming next, but strangely enough, he wasn't. His voice was steady and strong as he continued talking, and his knees didn't even tremble.

He guessed what the officer must be thinking. *How is it possible that this young man in the Russian army dares to speak of God? The Soviet Union is a Communist state with an atheistic political platform!* Did the colonel think Ivan was a visitor on the base? Not likely. Ivan was wearing his regulation gray-green military uniform. Did he think Ivan was unaware of the rules regarding the unofficial assembly of enlisted soldiers? Maybe. But the regulations for such misdemeanors were posted in the mess hall and in the barracks. Did he think Ivan had a death wish? Maybe, but then again, any soldier must be ready to face death on a daily basis.

The entire time Ivan was speaking, the colonel's clean-shaven face didn't scowl or even frown. He appeared steely-eyed and resolute, but he didn't interrupt Ivan. He didn't call a halt to the impromptu meeting, which had obviously become a disturbance in the regimented schedule of the military base. He just—sat and listened.

CHAPTER 10

He's *probably having every word written down,* Ivan mused to himself as he continued to preach. *Was the colonel gathering ammunition for what was sure to end up as a court-martial? Would he sentence Ivan to military prison, or banish him to a military outpost in the Siberian wastelands? Worse still, might he sentence Ivan to death before a firing squad?* Ivan had heard of such things happening. Men who were caught stealing in the army, or who fell asleep while on night watch, were often shot for these "crimes."

Ivan took a deep breath and gathered his wits about him. None of this mattered. A firm resolve to complete his task spurred him on to finish what he had started. He had laid everything out before the Lord and had thought things through clearly. If he were taken away to languish in some military outpost, it wouldn't matter. If he were shot, there would be others to tell the young soldiers in the army about the gospel. God would take care of everything.

If God's work for Ivan was already done in the short space of time he had been on the military base, then Ivan was satisfied. He was ready to do whatever God should ask of him next, and to go wherever He might lead.

However, if God's work for Ivan was only beginning, then all the cold in Siberia, all the generals in the military, all the bullets in the Soviet Union, could never stop him.

Then Ivan did what any good evangelist would do. He gave an altar call. Under the scrutinizing eye of the colonel on the training field of that military base in the heart of Moldova, Ivan gave an altar call!

It was really quite simple. Ivan's icy breath was causing frost to form on his nose and eyelashes, and a biting wind whipped his scarf around his neck and shoulders—but he ignored it all as he raised his hand and gave the call.

"My friends," he announced, "if you can hear God's voice speaking to you today, then open your heart and let Him fill your life with peace. He wants to show you a better way of life."

Of course, Ivan didn't really expect that anyone would actually come forward. Not really—by now every soldier standing on the military commons had to know that there was a high-ranking officer sitting in his jeep just a few yards behind them.

But then again, who could say? Someone might be brave enough to do such a thing at a time like this. Even if they didn't really know why they were responding to such a call, they might do it. Only God knew whether this might be the last time some of them would have a chance to hear the gospel invitation to accept Jesus and His gift of eternal life. The Holy Spirit might be at this very moment impressing some young man to accept the opportunity of a lifetime. Ivan had to give the call—he had to give the invitation! That was his job. He'd just have to leave the results to God.

There was a stir in the crowd, and then about a dozen young men made their way forward. Ivan smiled, congratulated them quietly on their choice, and then prayed for them in a clear strong voice. It wasn't a long prayer—just simple enough to introduce all the soldiers to the idea of prayer, and bold enough to let them know that he was not afraid to be a Christian.

"Our Father in heaven, thank You for another day of life. Thank You for the Fatherland and for the chance to serve in the Soviet Union army. Thank You for Jesus' death on the cross that has saved us from sin. O Lord, on this holy Sabbath day, help us to gratefully accept Your offer of eternal life. And now, please send Jesus soon, so that we can go home to live with You forever. In Jesus' name we pray, amen."

And that was it. There was no big tumult—no fanfare—no 16-gun salute. The whole thing ended as quietly as it had started. Within just a few minutes all the hundreds of soldiers had dispersed and Ivan was left standing alone on his box.

But of course the gray-green jeep was still there with the officer sitting in it. By now the driver had climbed back into the jeep and was awaiting further orders.

As Ivan stepped down off the cabbage crate, the colonel beckoned for him to come to the side of the jeep. From the moment he had stepped up on the crate Ivan's boldness had made him steadfast in his purpose, but now he suddenly felt his knees go weak. What would be the verdict? Had a judgment already been set against him?

It was a strange feeling, and he would never forget the sensation as long as he lived. His future was waiting in the balance, and there was nothing he could do about it.

Ivan slowly walked the few paces to the jeep, but he hadn't a clue what might happen next. The expression on the colonel's face remained as hard as stone. The lines etched there revealed many years of serving in the military. His eyebrows were prominent with bushy tufts of hair, and the man's steel-gray hair indicated he was older—maybe 55 or 56 years of age.

"What's your name, soldier!" the officer asked gruffly when Ivan had come as close as he dared.

"Gumenyuk, sir!" Ivan snapped to attention and fixed his eyes on some point beyond the officer.

"Gumenyuk!"

"Yes, sir!"

"Gumenyuk, you know that what you are doing here is forbidden!" The officer's words were more a statement than a question.

"Yes, sir!"

"Then why are you doing it?" he demanded.

"Because I've been called by God to be a missionary in the army." Ivan continued looking straight ahead, not daring to let his eyes wander. He could feel the colonel's eyes searing through him now like red-hot coals of fire.

There was an exaggerated pause as the colonel recoiled from Ivan's response. "You've been called to be a what?"

"To be a missionary, sir!"

"Well—I cannot allow you to be one of those—missionaries, whatever they are!" There was another long pause.

Ivan waited with bated breath. The colonel was toying with him. The dialogue could go in any of several different directions now, but it would probably have very little to do with what Ivan himself said. A punishment of some sort was in order, no doubt, but it did appear less and less that a firing squad was in the picture. Ivan allowed himself a glimmer of hope. Maybe the future wouldn't be as bleak as he had thought.

"This place operates on discipline and the traditions of the Soviet military," the colonel continued. "You must be willing to get in line and comply. Anything else will be considered an act of blatant insubordination."

"Yes, sir—I mean, no, sir!" Ivan blurted in confusion. "I mean, I cannot comply, sir!"

The officer drew back, startled at Ivan's blatant boldness. "You what!" he half shouted.

Ivan's heart began to beat faster! The conversation was beginning to spiral out of control. Things were not going well at all. His situation was not getting better—it was getting worse! He had thought that he might at least be given a chance to explain his reasons for preaching out on the military commons—but, then again, why should he be surprised? What did he expect? This was a military base, home of some 3,000 soldiers being trained in one of the fiercest armies on earth!

At that moment Ivan wanted to crawl down inside his shoes and never come out again. He had gotten himself into this mess—would he be able to get himself out? It didn't seem likely. Only God could save him now.

CHAPTER 11

Icannot comply, sir!" Ivan felt his stomach tighten and his mouth go dry. "Sir, in areas that have to do with my God, I cannot comply! I am willing to obey the laws of the land or the military, wherever I find myself, but when it comes to questions of my God, I must obey Him rather than men!"

Ivan stood stiffly at attention. He knew he didn't dare look in the colonel's direction. Military protocol denied him the right to do that, and besides, he didn't have the courage to do so at the moment anyway.

A chilly wind had sprung up again. Its sharp bite chilled Ivan, and he felt himself beginning to shiver. But it wasn't so much because of the cold as the tension of what might be coming next. Was he going to be court-martialed? Soldiers could be tried before a military court and then sentenced to hard labor for insubordination to superior officers. Ivan had heard of such a thing happening, but he had never thought that it could happen to him.

Ivan gulped. He was sure now that the colonel was not going to make it easy for him.

Ivan stood at attention waiting for the officer to speak again, but the silence was making him squirm. How long would he have to wait for a verdict? A minute? Two? It seemed like an hour before the colonel finally blurted, "Well, if that's the way you want it, then we're going to have to discuss this a bit further!" There was a pause, and then: "Report to my office at 1600 hours today."

Without another word he lifted his hand to the driver, and the jeep spun away across the military commons, sending a spray of snow into Ivan's face.

Ivan tucked his scarf into the collar of his coat and pulled his military cap down over his ears. He wrapped his arms around himself to calm his shivering body and then turned back to the barracks.

The colonel hadn't said what Ivan was supposed to do for the remainder of the day. Go to the field to drill with the other recruits? Show up at the kitchen for KP duty? Do 100 push-ups in the snow? If the situation hadn't been so serious, he might have laughed out loud, or even cracked a smile. But it *was* serious, and he was in a heap of trouble.

The officer hadn't given Ivan any further orders, which left him free to return to the barracks for the day. As he settled himself on his bunk a few minutes later, he breathed a prayer of thanksgiving to God.

"You've provided for me thus far, Lord—what's in store for me next? At 1600 hours I'll have to report to the colonel's office. Only You know what awaits me there." Ivan looked toward heaven. "But I guess that doesn't really matter right now, does it, Lord?"

He smiled to himself in the shadow of his bunk. At least he could now spend the Sabbath doing what he loved doing best—resting and praying. God was with him—there was no doubt about that. Hadn't he spent two hours in prayer just that morning? Hadn't the barracks been filled with the Spirit of God? Hadn't he been calmed by the promises in the Bible that God would be with him?

The day flew by, and before he knew it, 1600 hours had nearly arrived.

Ivan stood to his feet and stretched his muscles. He had been kneeling on the floor for so long that his knees had grown numb, and he was hungry besides. He had spent the day in prayer and forgotten to go to the mess hall.

No matter. Fasting had been good for him and had helped to give him the focus he needed.

Ivan pulled on his army coat and raised the collar to block the wind as he stepped out into the late-afternoon air. The temperature was dropping fast and he was glad that there was only a short distance between his barracks and the head office.

When Ivan arrived at the army base's administration offices, he told the company clerk in charge that he had arrived for his meeting with the colonel. Ivan sat on a bench in the hallway and waited nervously for the colonel to call him in.

The silence in the hallway was punctuated only by a clock ticking on the wall. To Ivan it sounded like a countdown to his sentence of doom. But the clock's hands seemed to stand still, and he was sure that there must be something wrong with it. And the longer he waited, the more nervous he became. What could be keeping the officer? When the clock read 1700 hours, Ivan was sure the colonel had forgotten all about him.

What should he do? Should he leave? Would anyone know that he had even showed up for his appointment?

At 1800 hours Ivan finally stood to his feet. He cleared his throat and timidly approached the company clerk. "Is this the place where the colonel's office is?"

"Colonel Ratovsky?"

Ivan shrugged. "I guess that's the right name."

"Well, you've got the right building, all right—but don't worry." The company clerk winked. "He makes young recruits wait quite a while sometimes." The clerk eyed Ivan curiously. "You're that new soldier in camp that was out lecturing to the recruits this morning, aren't you?"

Ivan looked at his feet for a moment and waited for words of condemnation, but they never came.

"That must have taken guts to do what you did," the clerk added. "Caused quite a stir, though. Everyone's been talking about you all day around here. The colonel came in growling late this morning and has been in his office all day." The clerk lowered his voice and threw a glance toward an imposing door behind him. "Maybe the colonel's fallen asleep. He does that sometimes."

Ivan didn't know whether to feel frightened or relieved—relieved that the officer might have nothing more important to do than sleep at his desk, but petrified of what he would say when he finally did wake up—if he was sleeping at all. Probably he had been on the radio all day talking with military headquarters somewhere, asking them what he should do with a young private who didn't know how to take orders on a Saturday morning.

The thought really frightened Ivan, but he didn't have long to mull it over, because the colonel's door suddenly opened. The company clerk stepped to the open doorway and saluted, spoke a few words to someone inside, and then motioned for Ivan to go in.

Ivan stood up and nervously twirled his army cap in his hand. This was it—time for the second showdown of the day, except that this time he probably wouldn't fare as well. This time the colonel would hand down his sentence. And this time there would be no delay of judgment.

Ivan stepped through the open doorway of the office. Inside, the colonel sat behind his desk in a wooden swivel chair, his back to Ivan. Facing the darkened window, the officer smoked quietly, looking out at the moon rising over the eastern horizon. A lone desk lamp cast a few rays of light in the dim room.

"Come in and take a seat," the officer grimly announced. "And close the door." His tone was neither harsh nor friendly.

"Sir?" Ivan hesitated for a moment. Had he heard right? He felt too nervous to sit in the presence of this officer who was about to hand down a sentence for military misconduct—but to disobey could only bring further trouble.

"Thank you, sir." Ivan settled himself stiffly in the straight-backed wooden chair opposite the colonel's desk and waited for the inevitable.

The officer's back was still turned to Ivan, but his solemn tone could mean only one thing. He was ready to send Ivan on his way: to the stockade or to a military tribunal that would be held at one of the military bases of the region—maybe the one in Kagul.

Ivan's mind began to race again. Worse yet, maybe he would be sent to work at a steel mill or a munitions factory in one of the closed cities of the Soviet Union. These legendary cities were famous for their secrecy—no one ever went in unless invited, and no one ever came out unless on military business.

"Do you want something to eat or drink? Tea, maybe?" Ivan was surprised that the colonel was acting hospitable. Could he possibly know that Ivan hadn't eaten all day?

Ivan looked at the tray sitting on the colonel's desk. On it was a bowl of borsch, a few thick slices of Russian bread, and a wedge of cheese. With all his heart Ivan wanted to accept the food, but something kept him from reaching out to take the bread. Did he dare trust the officer? What were the officer's intentions? Could the food be poisoned?

Ivan had no idea what might be in the food sitting there on the tray, but he was taking no chances.

CHAPTER 12

Ivan shivered in spite of the room's warmth. He had heard horror stories of soldiers mysteriously dying and of reports being sent home that these men had died of unfortunate circumstances in the line of duty.

Ivan shook his head in an attempt to clear his mind. Was he thinking rationally? Was there really danger of such a thing here in the colonel's office today? He couldn't tell, but one thing was sure—there was too much at stake right now to take that chance. Ivan wasn't concerned about himself so much—his life was in God's hands. But if the colonel was going to hear Ivan's Christian testimony, then Ivan had to be around to give it. A court-martial or even time in prison would be better than poison, but either way Ivan wanted to be ready and waiting when the opportunity to witness should arise.

"I'll not eat just now, sir," Ivan managed to finally stammer. "But thanks for the offer."

"Suit yourself," the officer grunted. There was another long moment of silence, leaving Ivan to wonder what was coming next. Ivan had been waiting all day for the officer's verdict, and now he was being made to wait yet again.

"So, Gumenyuk!" The officer continued, gazing out the window at the moon now rising swiftly over the horizon. "Tell me more about this God of yours."

Ivan momentarily froze at the request. He had been expecting a verdict on his crime of preaching, but he hadn't expected this. Tell the colonel more about God? Ivan wondered if he had heard the colonel clearly. Was this part of some grand scheme to get Ivan even further into trouble? Was the officer looking for more incriminating evidence that would condemn Ivan to the military stockade indefinitely?

Surely Ivan hadn't heard correctly! He tried to speak, but his voice caught in his throat. Finally he mustered the courage to stammer, "Please, sir—did I hear your question correctly?"

The colonel swiveled his chair around slowly and looked Ivan in the face. "You heard me correctly."

Ivan tried to gather his wits about him, but the officer was awaiting his reply. "Tell you about my God? Well, yes—there's so much to tell, and I guess you've caught me a bit off guard, sir!"

Ivan's head was fairly spinning as he realized that this would be an even greater test than the one he had faced earlier that morning. He had faced 3,000 soldiers and explained to them the gospel in a nutshell, but now he was being asked to spell it all out again—to lay it all out on the line for a commanding officer.

The officer sat quietly waiting, and Ivan couldn't stall much longer. Was the colonel being serious or cynical? Had there been a note of interest in the colonel's voice, or was this merely the calm before the storm? Ivan quickly sent a prayer heavenward.

"Help me, Lord! Tell me what to say! Only You know how much rides on my response to the colonel right now! Only You can give me the words I need to say that will be fitting."

Ivan took a deep breath and glanced at the officer. It was difficult to look him full in the face. As a colonel, he was Ivan's superior, a commanding officer in the army of the Soviet Union. But looking him in the eye seemed the right thing to do at the moment. Ivan might be a lowly recruit, just a simple private in the army, but he was also an ambassador for the God of the universe—the Creator of all things—the King soon to return in glory. This single fact seemed to be enough to put Ivan on equal footing with the colonel.

"My God is the one and only true God," Ivan began. "He has existed from time immemorial. Before there was time, there was God. My God created the universe and all that is in it—He has the power to speak merely a word, and what does not exist suddenly springs into existence.

"The Holy Scriptures say that when we look up at the night sky, we can see a marvelous display of God's craftsmanship." Ivan gestured toward the large window in the colonel's darkened office. "When God created the world for man, He took time to sprinkle the heavens with soft lights that would illumine the darkness. And He gave us the pale moon that races across the night sky."

The colonel turned toward the window to follow Ivan's panoramic description. He nodded his head slowly and then mumbled, "Imagine that! Sounds like a full day's work to me!"

Ivan smiled at the colonel's sense of humor and then added, "Actually, God did take one whole day to create the moon and stars—and the sun besides. The sun keeps us healthy with its life-giving rays. It keeps the cycles of our climate from becoming blistering hot or unbearably cold."

The colonel chuckled. "Unbearably cold, huh?"

Ivan smiled again. "Well, certainly not as cold as climates we might find on the moon or other planets in our solar system. After all, Colonel, eventually it does get warm again here in Moldova—something we can't say for the other side of the moon."

Ivan paused. "But that was just the fourth day of Creation, sir. In six days God created all that we see in this great world of ours. Moon, stars, the sun, the oceans and streams with their fish, the beautiful landscapes, trees and flowers, animals, birds—and humans, of course. Everything we see that causes us to wonder and delight in His awesome power—all of it was made for us to enjoy."

Ivan spoke with assurance now. He was beginning to relax. This was where he felt most comfortable—speaking of God's great power displayed in His incredible creative design.

But Ivan knew this was only one aspect of God's character. Speaking of God's power was the easy part. There was more, and for someone like the colonel, the picture might be harder to paint. Ivan couldn't tell whether the colonel was an atheist, an agnostic, or maybe someone just steeped in the traditions of a godless society. Just where the colonel's philosophy lay was anyone's guess. He was asking questions, but was he genuinely searching? Or did his questions stem from mere curiosity? For someone who was truly searching for truth, Ivan's explanations might make sense, but if not, they might just as easily backfire.

Ivan decided that none of this really mattered. Right now it was his job to share his testimony and be a missionary for God. The Holy Spirit would have to do the rest.

The hours sped by as Ivan went on to explain God's great love and compassion for the erring human race, how humanity fell from God's grace, and how God tried to keep the hope of salvation alive among human beings. Ivan shared about the story of Jesus coming to live on earth as a baby. He told of Jesus' death for all of humanity and of His resurrection three days later. Finally Ivan told the colonel of Jesus' commission that His followers go to all the world with the gospel, and that they tell everyone in every nation about the soon coming of Jesus.

"And that is why I must be a missionary man wherever I go," Ivan confessed. "Right now I'm in the army, so that's where I must be a missionary. Next year it may be someplace else. God will decide that for me."

By now it was late, and Ivan was tired. He had been up since 4:00 that morning, and now it was nearly midnight. Where had the time gone!

And he was hungry. He hadn't eaten all day. He now hungrily eyed the food still on the tray. He felt a bit sheepish for distrusting the colonel and the meal he had offered Ivan earlier in the evening.

The corners of the colonel's mouth twitched good-naturedly as he saw Ivan glancing at the tray. "Now would you like something to eat?"

Ivan didn't wait for a third invitation, but began eating the bread and cheese. "Here, let me heat the borsch for you," the colonel offered. A teakettle of hot water sat warming on a radiator along one wall, and the colonel poured some of the steaming water onto the red borsch. Before long the savory smell of onions and beets filled the room, and Ivan eagerly ate the borsch before settling back into his chair.

The two of them sat talking for quite some time about the life of a soldier in the army and the problems such a lifestyle could bring to a Christian young man. Ivan chuckled to himself at the thought of having such a pleasant conversation with this high-ranking military officer. The whole chain of events was amazing!

Before he knew it, the clock on the wall struck 2:00.

The colonel sat pondering all that Ivan had said. His eyes were closed, but Ivan could see a look of compassion cross his face.

Finally he stood to his feet. "The hour is late, and I know you need to sleep. I'm going to give you an infirmary pass for tomorrow," he offered. "Go directly to the infirmary now. That way you can sleep late without anyone asking you to report for roll call or drill practice.

They'll have a bed made up for you there." He winked at Ivan. "It's nice and warm in there. Tell them Colonel Ratovsky sent you."

And with that Ivan was pushed out the door. There was no time to really thank the officer for his hospitality. And besides, Ivan wasn't even really sure what had happened. Had a friendship started between the two of them? Ivan doubted it. Privates don't fraternize with colonels.

No doubt the next day everything would return to normal on the base—the colonel probably would not speak to Ivan in public. Behind closed doors was one thing, but on the military commons or during inspection, he would probably hardly remember Ivan. After all, Ivan was just one among thousands.

It didn't matter. Ivan was dead on his feet. He checked himself into the infirmary and fell exhausted into a warm, soft bed. Tomorrow was another day, and sleep was all Ivan wanted right now. Being a missionary in God's service might be his calling, but sleep was the next order of business.

CHAPTER 13

Ivan awoke to the smell of liniment. The odor was so strong that it almost made him ill. Where was he, and how had he gotten here? Sitting up on his cot, he looked around the large room. Then he remembered—he was in the infirmary.

The room contained a dozen army cots, some of which were occupied by soldiers, while others were empty. A few men in medical uniforms busied themselves making beds, dressing wounds, and dispensing medicines. But they all left Ivan alone.

Ivan closed his eyes and lay back down on the cot to soak up the warmth of the wood stove near his bed. A fire crackled inside, and a teakettle whistled merrily on the back of its dull surface.

The sun's long rays slanted in through the high window in front of him, but Ivan couldn't tell what time it was. Late morning? Early afternoon? Still a little drowsy, he wondered if he had really been in the colonel's office until 2:00 in the morning. The previous day seemed long ago and far away, as though it were part of some dream.

A wave of gratitude washed over Ivan for the way God had worked things out so far. Ivan suddenly felt the urge to roll out of bed and onto his knees to thank God properly, but then he remembered that he wasn't in his own bed in the barracks.

That was enough to get Ivan going for the day—he needed to be alone with God, and he certainly couldn't do it here. It was time to get back to army life.

Ivan sat up on the cot again, and swung his feet out over the side. "Do you have anything I could eat?" he asked one of the men. "I'm pretty hungry."

After a meal of boiled cabbage and bread, Ivan put on his coat and walked back to the barracks. It was now late afternoon, but none of the other recruits were back from their training exercises. Ivan wouldn't be expected to join the rest of the soldiers on the training field, so he used the spare time to get his personal things in order. His uniform needed to be pressed, his shoes shined, and his footlocker put in order. Then he decided to go to the army kitchen and help the cook get in a supply of wood, coal, and water. With his peculiar diet it would be wise to be on good terms with the head cook.

Later that evening Ivan was sitting on his bed reading his Bible when two MPs came into the barracks. "Gumenyuk!" they quietly demanded. "Come with us!"

Ivan looked from one MP to the other. "What's this all about?"

Their impassive faces gave him no clues. "We've just been told to bring you along. That's all."

Ivan followed the MPs out into the dark night, where he found an official car waiting for him. He was pushed into the back seat of the sedan and whisked away without further explanation.

In the front of the car beside the driver sat a distinguished-looking officer. He didn't speak to Ivan as they sped along the road, or even turn to acknowledge that Ivan had gotten into the car. He just sat smoking a cigarette and staring at the road ahead.

Ivan felt his pulse quicken as he looked at the officer and then at the driver. Where were these men taking him? What were they going to do with him? Sweat began to collect on his forehead, and he felt his hands beginning to tremble. Evidently he was in trouble—and there was no doubt in his mind that it had everything to do with his boldness in preaching to the 3,000 or so army recruits the morning before.

Perhaps he had been a little too brazen in his approach. Maybe he should have worked with the soldiers in smaller groups or even with lone individuals—Jesus had done that kind of thing in His ministry.

This problem was not going to go away easily. No doubt there would be a price to pay for preaching illegally the morning before.

As the car sped down the wintry road, Ivan now found himself wishing that he had counted the cost of his missionary efforts. Gone were the good feelings he had nurtured the night before while visiting with the colonel in his office. It had been a wonderfully refreshing witnessing experience, but it had been behind closed doors. Had he really thought that his visit with the colonel was the end of the incident on the military commons? Had he imagined that everyone would some-how be inspired with his naive method of evangelism?

And maybe this had nothing to do with the colonel anyway, no matter how much they had enjoyed talking into the wee hours of the morning. Probably someone higher up was responsible for Ivan being called out at this hour. They would certainly have heard about the late-night visit—there was no escaping the inevitable. Hadn't the company clerk told him that everyone on the military commons was talking about the incident? No doubt Ivan's brazen attempts at evangelizing the entire compound was now bringing down the wrath of the Soviet mil-itary command.

Ivan shook himself to clear his mind of such depressing thoughts. This was ridiculous! What was he thinking? Had he so soon forgotten his calling? He was a missionary man in the military. That was his goal, and had been ever since he had joined the army.

Ivan could feel the Spirit of God calming him down, and he took several deep breaths to regain his composure. It didn't matter what these men did with him. They could take him out to some secret mil-itary location and interrogate him regarding his faith if they wanted. They could mistreat him, abuse him, or put him in front of a firing squad. It didn't matter! Not really.

Ivan knew in his heart that God was with him there in the darkness of the night. Driving along a lonely country road on a cold winter night with strange men who might very well do him harm no longer held fear for Ivan. It was amazing! A feeling of peace had settled over him. Even if they should take his life, God would help him to be strong and true to his faith.

After about 20 minutes the driver turned the car off the main road and entered a narrow rutted trail through the forest. The ground was frozen hard, and at times, as they hit the ruts, the sedan would jump from one side of the road to the other. Ivan began to think that he probably wouldn't die at the hands of his interrogators—that he might die as the result of a collision with one of the trees on the side of the narrow road.

Finally they came to a small dacha huddled among the trees. Illuminated by the headlights, the place looked deserted. Ivan could see no trace of light in any of the windows of the small cabin.

Again Ivan wondered what would be done with him. Would they imprison him out here in this isolated location, where he could not continue to witness to the other soldiers?

The driver stopped the car in front of the dacha. He got out and opened the back door of the car for Ivan. Ivan hesitated only a moment—whatever lay inside the dacha had to be faced. "Please, Lord," he whispered, "keep me strong for You. Help me to think clearly so that I can speak as Your witness to all who will listen."

The officer led the way through the snow to the dacha, opened the door, and beckoned for Ivan to go inside. There was nothing Ivan could do but obey—there was no place else to go. He couldn't run, and he couldn't hide. It was time to stand up for Jesus and endure the consequences, whatever they might be.

CHAPTER 14

Inside, the dacha was pitch-black. There wasn't a light in the place anywhere. The officer led Ivan into an inner room, shut the door behind them, and pushed him into a chair. Ivan waited breathlessly while the officer struck a match and lit a lantern.

Ivan was stunned speechless at what he saw as the flickering light began to brighten the darkened room. Sitting in the room all around him were perhaps 20 army officers. He had been so apprehensive at being pushed into the darkness that he hadn't even sensed their presence in the room.

What were these officers doing here? The rank of each was evident by the medals and insignias they wore. There were captains and lieutenants and majors. Ivan's barracks sergeant was there, and so was Colonel Ratovsky.

Ivan was shocked at the sight of the colonel and the other officers, but the most eerie aspect of it all was that none of the officers spoke. A long moment of silence hung thick in the air as Ivan glanced around the room. What could they all possibly be doing here? Had they all come to interrogate him? Had they come to witness his execution at the hands of a firing squad?

Most of the officers were smoking cigarettes and drinking vodka. Finally one of them stood to his feet, stepped toward Ivan, and extended a pack of cigarettes. "We are sorry to have troubled you at this hour," he apologized. "Would you care for a cigarette?"

Again Ivan didn't know what to say. Was this all a game? Were these officers toying with him? He braced himself for the mistreatment he knew must follow.

The officer continued holding out the pack of cigarettes to Ivan.

Ivan finally found his voice. "Um, thank you. I mean, no thank you—I don't smoke."

"Would you like a drink, then?" The officer was insistent as he extended the glass of vodka he held in his hand. "My name is Alexander."

Ivan hesitated. "I'm sorry," he stammered. "I don't drink, either."

Alexander grinned and sat back in his chair. "And what *do* you do, private?"

Ivan stared at Alexander in the dim light cast by the solitary lantern, and then at the other officers sitting nearby. He knew he needed to start talking. If these men were playing games with him, he might as well give them something to talk about. It was now or never.

"I'm a witness for Jesus," Ivan managed to say. "I'm a missionary for Him, and I spread the good news of the gospel. That is what I do."

Alexander eyed Ivan intently. "Tell us about this gospel," he added as he snuffed out his cigarette in an ashtray.

All eyes were on Ivan now.

"The good news is that God loves each one of you." Ivan felt the Holy Spirit speaking through him. "Even before you and I were born, God knew what we would look like. He knew the very number of hairs we would have on our heads. He knew what our dreams and hopes would be, the troubles we would face, and the lives we would lead."

Ivan looked from one face to the next in the room full of silent men. "God knows we are all sinners—there is none among us that is good. He knows that since we are sinful men, we will all have to die an eternal death of darkness—but He has a plan that can save us."

Ivan paused to let his words sink in.

"Go on," Alexander urged.

"We were not made for this wicked world of pain and suffering, and God doesn't want us to have to stay here. He offers each of us a choice—we can choose His way, or we can choose the road that leads to death."

Alexander nodded. "This God of yours? He makes the rules?"

"Yes!" Ivan nodded his head slowly. "He makes the rules. He has always been in charge, and He always will be."

Several of the officers looked at one another, and then one man with slate-gray eyes leaned forward. "I do not understand," he began.

"If your God is in charge of this world with His plan, how come there is so much bad in it?" The officer raised his eyebrows. "Why do we have wars—and killing? Does this God of yours like killing?" He looked around self-consciously, and then added sheepishly, "I do not want to offend you or your God. I just want to know."

All the men had stopped smoking and drinking by now, and several murmured their agreement.

Alexander nodded his head. "Those questions have bothered me, too. My mother attended the Russian Orthodox Church in our village for years, and I was always afraid when she talked about God's anger and wrath.

"But now, tonight, you are saying that your God is a God of love and that He wants to offer us life." He paused and thought for a moment. "So if your God cares about us, as you say, then why are there famines? Why do people die of horrible diseases, and why do criminals go unpunished by God? If your God knows everything and sees everything, why doesn't He punish the criminals and help those who suffer?"

Ivan was amazed, but he kept his composure. These men were asking all the classic questions that could be explained only by telling them the story of the war between good and evil, the great controversy between God and Satan. Ivan recognized that the answers to their hard questions wouldn't necessarily convince them all, but at least he would have a chance to tell them what they needed to hear most.

"Well, first of all," Ivan began, "this God we speak of is not my God alone. He's your God too. He's everybody's God. He created all men, so we are all His sons. And second," Ivan continued, "He isn't the one that brings evil. It is Satan who is to blame—the one who was once called Lucifer."

"Lucifer?" Alexander wondered aloud.

Ivan nodded his head slowly and gazed into the lantern's glowing flame. "Long ago and far away, before this world was made, there was harmony and peace from one end of the universe to the other. Worlds like ours revolved in their orbits. The solar systems and galaxies followed their pathways. Everything was in its place. All creation pulsed in one glad rhythm of life and thankfulness for God's goodness and love. There was no death or killing. Life existed to support life, and all created life lived to bless God. From the greatest world to the tiniest atom, all life existed with the purpose of bringing happiness and balance to God's vast creation spread across the unlimited reaches of space.

"But Lucifer—an angel created by God, and the most powerful of all the creatures in the universe—became jealous of the power of God and His Son, Jesus. They were designing a new world that was soon to be created—our world, the earth—and Lucifer demanded that he be allowed to help in the plans and creation of it." Ivan looked around at the men. Every face was turned toward him expectantly.

"But the awesome act of creating a world belongs to God," Ivan continued, "and no created being has the right to demand such a thing of God. Sadly enough, Lucifer eventually turned against God and poisoned the minds of many in heaven. Because of his insane jealousy there was war in heaven, and Lucifer was cast out of heaven, taking with him all those who had rebelled against God."

"Cast out? Where did he go?" asked a chorus of voices.

"He went to other worlds, and then he finally came here to our earth after it had been created. So, you see, it is he who has brought trouble and conflict to this world."

Ivan went on to share the story of humanity's fall in the original garden of Paradise. He told of God's chosen people down through the centuries who were entrusted with God's law, but who fell from grace time and again. And he told of Jesus' sacrifice on the cross to give us a chance to return to that garden of Paradise.

The chilly darkness pressed in on the little group that cold winter's night, but the small ring of light from the lantern bravely sent its faint glow into the furthest corners of the room. And like the light, Ivan's stories brought a glimmer of hope to the men. It stirred their hearts like nothing ever had before.

And so the night went. Sometime before dawn Ivan was finally taken out to the car and back to the army base. Again he was sent to the infirmary so he could catch up on his sleep. As he settled into his bed by the woodstove, his heart sang in praise to the God he had pledged to witness for as a missionary.

Why had God chosen Ivan to be His witness at the army base? Why Ivan, a boy from an obscure village in the middle of Moldova? There had been very little sacrifice on Ivan's part—as of yet—and certainly no suffering to speak of. No severe interrogations, no forced labor in the stockade. No persecution for his faith, unless being compelled to stay up all hours of the night could be considered persecution.

Ivan had been sure that witnessing for God would bring out all the devil's big guns, but thus far it had brought only spiritual satisfaction and incredible opportunities to tell others about Jesus.

In just two days Ivan had gone from being a mere private who was worried about Sabbath privileges to being called before a "tribunal" of atheistic Soviet officers who had suddenly become interested in the gospel of Jesus Christ.

What an amazing turn of events! Who would have believed that such a thing could happen? And who knew what tomorrow would bring?

CHAPTER 15

Late that afternoon Ivan was called to Colonel Ratovsky's office again.

The colonel welcomed him in warmly. "Things surely have picked up with you around here, Gumenyuk. There's not been a dull moment in the last three days." He gestured toward a chair. "Have a seat, private—cigarette?" He extended a pack of cigarettes, but Ivan held up his hand.

"No, thank you, sir. I mean, thank you, sir, but I don't smoke."

"You don't smoke?" Colonel Ratovsky squinted at Ivan from beneath bushy eyebrows. "Well—now that you mention it, I guess you didn't smoke last night at the dacha, either. Why not?"

Ivan grinned. "Well, I've never tried to smoke, but I can't imagine that it would be much fun."

"But all men smoke. Don't you want to be a man?"

At 18 Ivan knew he was still considered a boy by most men in the military, both officers and recruits alike.

"To be honest, actually, I don't smoke because God has asked that I treat my body as His temple—a place where He can dwell."

The colonel looked perplexed. "So your God lives inside of you?"

"Spiritually, yes. His power fills me to help me be His witness."

"I've never heard anything so strange in all my life." The colonel continued puffing on the cigarette sticking out one side of his mouth.

Again Ivan only smiled.

The colonel continued puffing on his cigarette, all the while contemplating what Ivan had said. "Well, anyway, that's not why I called you here this afternoon, Gumenyuk. I called you in to see if you have everything you need."

"Sir?"

"I wanted to be sure that you are comfortable. Is the army treating

70

you right? A private leads a pretty simple life and certainly doesn't have all the comforts of home."

"I have everything I need, sir. Thank you."

"Can I interest you in anything special in the way of food? I have access to whatever you might need."

Ivan kept smiling, but only shook his head.

The colonel stared at Ivan and scratched his head. "Gumenyuk, you are a most unusual boy. Any other soldier called in here would be asking me for all kinds of favors. A stash of vodka for their footlocker—special meats and cheeses—a weekend pass to town." He took the cigarette from his mouth and shook his head, as though waiting for Ivan to break down and finally make some special request.

Ivan couldn't think of anything he needed. His mother and father had taught him to be grateful for what he had and never to take advantage of a good thing simply because someone was offering it.

"You never know when someone might be offering you something for the sake of their own personal gain," his father had said. Ivan saw the wisdom in those words and didn't want to become indebted to the colonel. Right now he needed to stay as free from obligations as possible.

Suddenly Ivan remembered his worries about Sabbath observance. That had been his greatest concern when he first arrived on the army base, and now he realized that this might be his opportunity to let the colonel know of his convictions.

Today was Monday. The Sabbath would be coming again in just five days. Because of the way things had turned out on the previous Sabbath, just two days before, he hadn't needed to make his petition known. He had inadvertently received the day off because he had been sent to the barracks by the colonel.

"All right, then," Ivan finally said, looking straight at Colonel Ratovsky. "If you want to do something for me, please let me have every Subbota off. That way I can worship God properly, as He has asked me to do."

The colonel merely squinted at Ivan again, as though not comprehending what Ivan had said. "You want to worship your God? Every Subbota? Where will you do that? We have no temple or church here." The colonel put out another cigarette. "You are truly a peculiar boy,

Gumenyuk. Why have you not said something about this before?"

Ivan hesitated. "I guess with all the commotion I caused last Sabbath, I forgot to talk about that being one of the reasons I was preaching to the soldiers."

"Sabbath? What's this Sabbath you talk of? I thought it was Subbota you wanted off." The colonel's face was even more puzzled now.

"The seventh day of the week is the Sabbath, or Subbota, as everyone calls it in Russian. Sabbath is the word the Bible uses for Subbota. The Bible says that God made the seventh day holy. He did it to celebrate His creation of this world in six days. And now He asks that we keep this day, the Sabbath, holy by not working on that day—we are to spend time with Him in prayer and Bible study."

The colonel's face grew thoughtful. "Amazing!" he exclaimed. "All these years the word *Subbota* has been staring me in the face, and I never thought about it that way. So," he quickly added, "you want me to arrange for you to have your Sabbath off—in the army?"

Ivan held his head high. "Yes, sir."

"The Soviet army?"

Ivan's face broke into a boyish grin.

"Do you know what you are asking, Gumenyuk?"

"I think so, sir."

"Well, I will see what I can arrange." The colonel nodded good-naturedly. "Will that be all, private?"

"That's everything I can think of—for now, at least."

The colonel stared at Ivan suspiciously. "There's more, isn't there?" He shook his head incredulously. "Tell me there isn't more!"

"Well, sir—there is one other thing." Ivan paused and glanced toward the door. "Do I need to come back another time, sir?"

"No—no, let's get this over with now." The colonel grunted and then began to chuckle. "I thought I had heard everything when you told me you don't smoke, and now this Sabbath day thing!"

Ivan leaned forward in his chair.

"So, out with it, young man. What else do you need?"

"Sir—could you make arrangements for me not to have to carry a gun?"

The colonel raised his eyebrows. "A gun? What's the matter with our guns?"

"It's not that—actually, I'm a Seventh-day Adventist Christian, and Seventh-day Adventist young men are taught not to kill. So I'd like to ask that I be excused from field exercises with a gun."

The colonel began to sputter, as if trying not to laugh. "No target practice? Whatever will you come up with next, private?"

"I could be a medic," Ivan quickly offered. "That's what I signed up for. Or I could serve in the kitchen." He wanted to make this as easy for the colonel as he possibly could.

The colonel rolled his eyes playfully. "All right, Gumenyuk—these arrangements could create problems for me here on the base, but I'll see if I can arrange something."

Ivan was amazed at the ease with which each of these problems was dispatched. He had anticipated real trials in the army on both of these issues—the Sabbath and not wanting to carry a gun. There would be trials ahead, no doubt, but for now God surely was taking care of the roadblocks one by one.

"Thank you, sir." Ivan bowed his head. "You are too kind."

"Don't mention it, Gumenyuk." The colonel rolled his eyes again. "Now, there's something I need you to do for me." The lines on his forehead tightened.

"If it's in my power, sir."

"It is." The colonel's voice grew serious. "I want you to stop preaching to the soldiers on this army base."

Now it was Ivan's turn to be surprised. His mouth dropped in protest. "No more preaching?"

"No preaching—not in public. For one thing, I can't have crowds of soldiers causing a commotion the way they did last Subbota—or Sabbath, as you call it. And second, allowing a Christian on this military base to preach about God, who we claim doesn't exist, can only throw the philosophy of the Soviet army into disarray. Can you imagine the trouble I'd be in if the brass up in Moscow should hear of this?"

"But—but, I have to preach," Ivan countered. "I was called to the army to speak for God. I'm His witness on this base."

"Not in public, you aren't." The colonel was firm. "If you must speak of your God—and I know you will—do it in the barracks in the evenings with small groups or with the men one-on-one."

Ivan nodded his head slowly. "Yes, sir."

The colonel took a deep breath. "Now, if there's nothing else you need, Gumenyuk?"

Ivan got to his feet and started toward the door.

"Oh, and Ivan—one more thing." The colonel eyed Ivan warily. "Everything we have talked about here is off the record. I think that would be best. Last night at the dacha—and the night before that, here in this office—we never had these conversations." He smiled again and scratched his chin. "Do I make myself clear?"

Ivan didn't miss a beat. "Yes, sir! Not a problem, sir."

The colonel lowered his voice. "I mean, it wouldn't do for the rest of the base to know about these—meetings. Would it?

"Absolutely—not, sir!"

"All right, then. That will be all, private." With a wave of his hand the colonel dismissed the boy.

CHAPTER 16

During the next few days Ivan returned to the usual regimen of training with the other recruits. Late Thursday afternoon he was once again summoned to the colonel's office.

"At ease, private," the colonel smiled. "I've arranged for your transfer to the medical unit—that way you won't have to train with a gun. But you may have to carry one should your unit be sent to the front lines somewhere." He looked up from the paperwork at his desk. "You do know how to use a gun, don't you, Gumenyuk?"

"Yes, sir," Ivan replied, "but, sir—I'd rather not."

"I understand, private, but this is the best I could do right now. The lieutenant of the medical corps agreed to take you on provided your gun is kept with the unit for field exercises." The colonel noticed Ivan's look of disappointment. "Trust me, private, you'll never have to use it. It's a mere formality."

Ivan nodded gratefully.

The colonel got up and walked over to the tall shelves lining one wall of his office. "Do you read much, Gumenyuk?"

"Yes, sir. A little, sir."

"Then I'll let you look through the volumes I have. I've got some choice volumes here by Tolstoy, Pushkin, Marx."

A look of surprise crossed Ivan's face.

"I trust you, Ivan."

The sun had set, and the colonel's office was growing dim in the gathering evening shadows. Colonel Ratovsky turned on his desk lamp. "Go ahead, private. You may choose some volumes now if you'd like and simply return them when you're finished."

Ivan was ecstatic. With a feeling akin to reverence he moved toward the bookshelves. That he should find such classics on a military base was amazing, he thought, but to be offered a chance to read them—that was even more astounding. Ivan was overwhelmed and truly humbled that the colonel trusted him with his own personal property.

"Thank you, sir" was all Ivan managed to stammer.

"Not a problem, Gumenyuk."

As Ivan scanned the titles on the shelves, the colonel reached into a low cabinet behind his desk. He brought out a bottle of vodka and two glasses. "Gumenyuk, I see good days ahead for you. You are bright, hardworking, and a born leader. And you are a man of integrity. We value these traits. I'm going to recommend you for a promotion."

"A promotion?" Ivan turned to the colonel.

"A promotion. I need young men like you. I'd like to recommend that you go through special officers' training."

Surprised again, Ivan's mouth dropped open.

"Don't be so surprised, private. I'm sure you know we've been watching you. I must admit it's rare indeed that we find someone so soon in the screening process. It's been, what—two weeks since you've arrived? Not even that, I guess, and already you are making us stand up and take notice."

Ivan continued to stare at the colonel. Was this all a dream? Was he hallucinating?

Colonel Ratovsky extended a glass of vodka to Ivan. "I want to propose a toast to the best young recruit to arrive on this base, since— I don't remember."

"Thank you," Ivan stammered appreciatively. "I—I don't know what to say."

He tried to comprehend fully what the colonel was saying—tried to gather his wits. So much was happening so fast. What was he to do? Had he heard the colonel correctly? It was an incredible opportunity to be offered a promotion, and so soon. He had never envisioned himself as an officer in the Soviet military. How did one go about doing that as a Christian?

Suddenly Ivan realized that Colonel Ratovsky was still holding out the glass of vodka to him. "Oh, sir—I'm sorry, but—but I don't drink—sir."

Now it was the officer's turn to be surprised again. "You don't drink?" The colonel's face lost some of its candor. "Aren't you feeling well?" Colonel Ratovsky glanced at the bottle of vodka on his desk. "Is it the brand you don't like? I'm sorry about that, but it's the only kind I have." He scrutinized Ivan's face. "I guess I could get some wine from the kitchen, if you'd prefer. Is this stuff too strong for you, Gumenyuk?"

Ivan lost his nerve for a moment. How could he refuse the drink Colonel Ratovsky was offering him? It was a token of the man's offered friendship. It was an effort to reach out and bridge the gap between an officer and an enlisted army recruit. It appeared to be a genuine gesture from a man who was attempting to take Ivan under his wing.

But Ivan had never drunk alcohol before. Even if it had been the right thing to do—and he knew it wasn't—Ivan wouldn't have been able to stomach the vodka. He would have vomited it up for sure and that wouldn't have done anything for his image in a man's army.

But of course none of that really mattered. Ivan could never drink the alcohol. He had been raised to respect his parents, his church, and his conscience.

In that fleeting moment, standing there before the colonel holding the glass of vodka in his outstretched hand, Ivan remembered Daniel. It was the stories of Daniel that had inspired Ivan and his friends to be missionaries for God. He and his friends had spoken of those ancient tales so many times that it was part of who they were. Daniel was a man of principle, a true missionary—and they had all wanted to be like him.

Ivan smiled to himself in the dim light. Daniel would have known what to do in this situation—and Ivan knew what he must do.

He took a deep breath. "Thank you, sir, but I cannot accept the drink. It wouldn't be right before God, and it wouldn't honor the promise I made to my parents long ago. My body is the temple of God, and for the same reasons I cannot smoke, I cannot drink, either."

Colonel Ratovsky shook his head, and then he started laughing. In fact, he laughed so hard and so long that Ivan began to feel embarrassed. Ivan's face flushed red—he was sure the company clerk would come in to find out what the commotion was all about, and then he would be doubly embarrassed.

"No! No! Gumenyuk! I'm not laughing at you!" The colonel accidentally sloshed some of the vodka onto the floor from the two shot glasses he held in his hands. "Well, I guess I am laughing at you, but it's not out of ridicule, my boy. It's out of sheer surprise at finding someone who is so stubbornly true to his convictions, even if I don't hold those ideals myself. And it's admiration for the devotion you have for your God," he added soberly.

The officer set the shot glasses down on his desk. "Gumenyuk! For a man who knows his own mind, I'd take your peculiar ways any day of the week. I guess that's why I like you so much."

Again Ivan didn't know what to say, but he was grateful to God for the way things had worked out. What could he say? He had made the right decision and had stayed true to his conscience. *Thank You, Lord,* Ivan prayed silently. *You have been with me once again to help me make the right choices and witness for You in spite of my fears.*

The two men had a good laugh over the whole incident, and then, after putting the vodka back into the liquor cabinet, Colonel Ratovsky came around the corner of his desk and put his arm across Ivan's shoulder.

"Gumenyuk, I want to make this up to you. I'd like to offer you something you would enjoy." He laughed again and then added, "You don't smoke and you don't drink. How about something to eat, then? A favorite type of food, maybe?"

Ivan grinned. "Prianieki," he replied without hesitation. "Like my mother makes—I love her prianieki sweet cake."

The colonel smiled broadly and slapped Ivan on the shoulder. "Say no more, my boy. You shall have it."

That evening with the colonel was the beginning of a real friendship between the two men. Ivan no longer feared the officer, rough though he seemed at times. The man was becoming something of a father figure to him, and he sensed that the colonel needed something from him, too. Not just a young man of integrity on his army base, but someone in whom he could confide, someone who would say what he was really thinking, regardless of the outcome.

And now little perks for Ivan began to appear, things Ivan knew few men on the base had access to. One evening he opened his footlocker to find the prianieki he had asked for. Another night it was a block of feta cheese wrapped in paper. Ivan felt a bit guilty for receiving such gifts and even more awkward for accepting them. It didn't seem right that he should receive special treatment when all he wanted was to be a missionary and share the gospel story with the other soldiers on the base.

And then one Friday afternoon in February, Ivan was called to the colonel's office. After their usual greetings, Colonel Ratovsky beckoned for Ivan to follow him. Leaving the building, he led Ivan across the army base to the officer's quarters and opened the door to a well-furnished apartment. Plush upholstered chairs and couches graced the front room, and there was a large colorful mohair carpet on the floor in front of a cozy fireplace. A smaller room off the front room boasted a polished mahogany desk and a wall lined with books.

"This is for you," the colonel proudly announced. "It's a room fit for a man of your caliber, Gumenyuk."

Ivan opened his mouth in an exclamation of protest, but Colonel Ratovsky lifted his hand to silence the boy. "We'd like for you to become an officer," he insisted. "And to get the process going, we're promoting you to the rank of sergeant—I'll not have my officers living in quarters that are beneath their dignity.

"And now I must be going," the colonel quickly added. "Enjoy your new living arrangements, son, and enjoy your Sabbath day tomorrow." The man said the words almost reverently and then shut the door, leaving Ivan to wonder at the goodness of God.

Ivan dropped to his knees in thanksgiving. His blessings were full to overflowing! Surely things could not get any better for him than they already were!

CHAPTER 17

Sabbath was a paradise for Ivan as he basked in the comfort of his new rooms. Like the colonel's books, the volumes in his personal library couldn't be read during Sabbath hours—there wasn't a religious one among them. But the fire in his fireplace was pleasant, and Ivan found plenty of time to lounge by its cheerful flames while he read his Bible. He even had time to feel a little bit guilty again for receiving such treatment.

But Ivan was somewhat unsure as to what this new arrangement might cost him. He had never fully agreed to Colonel Ratovsky's plan to make him into an army officer. Furthermore, Ivan was still not sure why the colonel considered him to be officer material.

Ivan had always felt that his greatest gifts were that of a lay pastor working with common folks like the ones in his little village of Hitreshety. On the other hand, he couldn't deny that God was leading in all that he had experienced so far in the army. It was obvious to Ivan that God wanted him to share the gospel with as many enlisted soldiers as possible.

But did that involve becoming an army officer? Quite frankly, he had never thought of himself as fulfilling the gospel commission by becoming an officer. Would being an officer give him even more access to the enlisted men? It might, but then that was only one argument in favor of becoming an officer. There had to be disadvantages to receiving promotions of rank. Maybe his hands would be tied even more than they were now. Colonel Ratovsky had already forbidden him from speaking to the men in large groups.

That meant that any Bible studies Ivan wanted to give would have to be in small groups in the barracks either at night or early in the morning. Ivan was now studying with three men in the evening after the lights went out.

If Ivan stayed in the officers' quarters, would that mean that he would no longer have access to the men in the barracks? Would the men even want to associate with him at all? If that was the case, Ivan was sure he would rather not become an officer. The loss of spiritual time with the men would be too great a price.

But then again, maybe Ivan was worrying for nothing. Maybe he wouldn't even have a choice about whether or not he wanted to become an officer. Maybe he would simply have to do as he was told. Everyone had to obey orders, even officers. There was always a superior officer somewhere giving orders from the top.

Ivan wavered between these arguments all Sabbath. By sundown he had decided that he would decline Colonel Ratovsky's offer, including its benefit of having a sumptuous apartment.

But in the mess hall the next day Ivan received another surprise. He was eating with Dimitri and Sergei when a messenger showed up with instructions that Ivan was to accompany Colonel Ratovsky to an evening function. "Be ready by 1800 hours in your best uniform," the messenger warned.

"What does he want with you?" asked Sergei.

Ivan shrugged. Who could tell what Colonel Ratovsky might come up with next? Ivan had never told Sergei and Dimitri of the meetings with the colonel in his office or the secret rendezvous with the other officers in the dacha. He didn't want to betray the trust Colonel Ratovsky had put in him.

And he didn't want to spoil things for Sergei and Dimitri. Like Ivan, they were currently studying with men in their own units. Ivan didn't want them to lose that privilege by getting them involved in the confidential business of his own situation.

"Well, I guess I'll find out soon enough" was all Ivan could say.

He went to the barracks to brush his dress uniform. He had no idea what the colonel had up his sleeve, but a strange feeling of excitement and expectation came over him.

"Please, Lord," Ivan whispered as he took his khaki pants from between the boards he had used to press them the night before. "Help me to be ready for whatever You have in store tonight."

At the appointed time, an ominous-looking military car showed up to take Ivan to the "function." When the car pulled up to the door of a warehouse several kilometers away, Ivan was a little concerned. From the outside the place looked almost abandoned, but as soon as Ivan stepped inside, he saw that it was far from abandoned. The warehouse was actually a military facility and was the site of a lavish banquet for high-ranking army officials.

Colonel Ratovsky cheerily greeted Ivan after he was ushered into the lavish banquet hall. "I'm glad you graciously accepted my invitation to attend, Gumenyuk."

Ivan merely grinned, knowing full well that he never really had a say in the matter.

He was surprised at the extravagant surroundings, though, and a bit apprehensive as to what might be expected of him as the night wore on. To his relief, Ivan was allowed to remain in the background, although he did sit with the colonel.

The meal served was the best that the Soviet government could provide. Not surprisingly, Ivan found that he had to pick and choose from the many delicacies offered at the banquet.

It seemed that every type of food imaginable was spread out on the heavily loaded, elegantly decorated banquet tables. There were pastries and sautéed vegetables, candied fruits, and a dozen kinds of bread. Ivan was sure that much of what he was seeing was imported. Even when he asked one of the waiters the names of some of the foods, he still didn't recognize them.

And of course there were all kinds of meats. Hams and great platters of beef and lamb were scattered across the tables of the banquet hall. There were game birds of every sort and all types of fish, some of which Ivan had never seen before.

The whole picture reminded Ivan of the foods served Daniel when he was asked to eat at Nebuchadnezzar's table in Babylon. Of course, unlike Daniel and his three friends, Ivan could refuse these foods without risk of punishment, but it wasn't easy. Every time the colonel offered him something new to try, Ivan always had to ask what it was. And always the colonel assured him that it was all good food. Ivan would smile and then give a mini health lesson from the Bible as to why some of the foods were not good for the human body.

Ivan was afraid that the colonel would be offended, but he never was. He would only nod his head and smile.

But the most challenging part of the whole evening was the dilemma Ivan faced when everyone began drinking the wine and vodka. Ivan stuck out like a sore thumb, since it appeared that he was the only one not drinking alcohol.

Once or twice Colonel Ratovsky came to Ivan's aid to make an explanation for his special diet and why he wasn't drinking the alcohol. However, Ivan also had a ready answer that made sense and seemed logical.

One high-ranking officer was especially impressed with Ivan. *Who is this promising young man in the Soviet army?* he wondered.

He finally introduced himself. "So this is the one we have been hearing about!" He extended his hand to Ivan. "My name is General Shevchenko. I wish to understand what it is that can make a man who is so young stand so firm for the beliefs of his religion and home."

Ivan couldn't tell what direction the general was going with his questions, but he realized that what he said could make or break his case with the officers higher up the chain of command.

"Sir," Ivan began, "in matters that relate to the Fatherland, my allegiance is unwavering. I will go anywhere and serve with anyone who stands for the building of a strong future for the Soviet Union." Ivan paused momentarily, took a deep breath, and then quickly added, "However, when the regulations of my country clash with the laws of my God, I must obey my God. There can be no conflict between the two."

The general studied Ivan's face seriously. "Does that include the regulations of your army?"

Without flinching, Ivan looked straight at the general. "I believe it does."

By now everyone near Ivan had stopped eating and visiting among themselves and had turned to listen to this unusual conversation between a high-ranking general and a newly enlisted soldier. A deathly silence fell over the room for a few moments. Then the general put out his hand and grasped Ivan's. "You're an unusual young man, Gumenyuk. You've got courage, and confidence—I like your style."

Turning to Colonel Ratovsky, General Shevchenko nodded his head in Ivan's direction, "Hang on to this one, Ratovsky. He's a keeper."

"I'm doing the best I can, sir" was all the colonel would say, and Ivan could vouch for that.

CHAPTER 18

The rest of the evening went by in a blur. By midnight Ivan was back in his apartment, reflecting on the amazing event. It seemed that everywhere he turned military personnel were waiting to learn about God! How could this be in a nation of proclaimed atheists? How could it be happening in an army that was designed to promote a "survival of the fittest" mentality?

Things did not calm down much for Ivan during the next few weeks either. Twice more he was asked to come to the darkened dacha in the woods for a Bible study. And now, from officers up and down the chain of military command, he began receiving invitations to attend political rallies and military banquets.

"I hope the brass at the top don't get any bright ideas about stealing you away," Colonel Ratovsky muttered to Ivan one day.

Ivan laughed at the colonel's concern. "What would they want with me? I'm just a lowly private."

"Not anymore you aren't," the colonel smiled. "A week ago I put your name in for a promotion—and I just received word today that the promotion came through. You're going to be a lieutenant."

All Ivan could do was grin. He didn't know what to think—going from private to lieutenant was quite a jump! Too much was happening to him too fast!

"By the way, Gumenyuk, I've been meaning to ask you," the colonel added. "Have you got a girl?"

"Yes, sir—at home, sir."

"Well, have you proposed to her yet?"

Ivan looked a bit surprised and then sheepishly stammered, "N-n-no, sir."

"Well, why don't you marry the girl and bring her here to the base?

I think we could make her feel welcome." The colonel smiled knowingly.

"Yes, sir, I'm sure you could." Ivan blushed in his boyish way. "I'll give it some thought, sir."

Ivan did give the colonel's suggestion some thought. In fact, he decided to pass the "suggestion" along to Vera. In his wildest dreams he had never thought that bringing Vera to the army base was a possibility—that they could even hope to get married this soon. It was not unusual for a young man of Ivan's age to consider marriage. Many young people in Moldova were already married by 19 or 20 years of age.

Ivan would love to have Vera near him again, and be married besides. But would she think it was a good idea?

In his next letter to her he finally gathered enough courage to pop the inevitable question. As he waited for her to respond, he anxiously wondered if she was ready for the next step in their friendship. Would she be willing to become his wife?

She didn't keep him waiting long for a response. After a few weeks of prayer, a letter arrived on the base that made Ivan's heart sing.

Ivan requested a home leave pass so that he and Vera could make plans together. On the day of his leave an unusual car showed up at the door to his apartment. It was a maroon-colored American-made Chrysler Continental coupe, and Ivan wondered at the change in transportation. As of late, his transportation to and from the base was always in one of the black military vehicles reserved for officers.

Ivan asked the driver to stop by Colonel Ratovsky's office before leaving the base for the train station. "Nice car," Ivan crowed.

"So you like it?" Colonel Ratovsky laughed. "It just arrived yesterday. Specially delivered for me, and I thought you might like riding in it to the train station."

"You are too kind," Ivan exclaimed.

"Not a problem, Gumenyuk. Men like you and I need a car—it gives us the prestige we need so that our men will respect us." He gave Ivan a knowing wink. "You can use it any time you want."

Ivan's mouth dropped open for at least the hundredth time since he had first arrived on the army base.

"Don't look so surprised, Gumenyuk! You know what my plans are for you! Which brings me to another bit of news." The colonel laid a hand on Ivan's shoulder. "I've put your name in for another promotion."

"Another promotion!" Ivan gulped. "I didn't think a soldier could get promoted again so soon."

"Well, it won't come right away. You're not eligible to become a captain for another three months, but I've asked the brass to speed it along, and sometimes they make exceptions. We're trying to push you along through the ranks as fast as possible." The colonel grinned again. "They're pretty impressed with you—we'll see what happens."

"But I'm in the army to be a missionary, not an officer," Ivan humbly protested. "I've thought it over, and I don't see how I can do both."

"Well, don't worry about that right now," Ratovsky assured him. "Go home, and give it some thought while you're there."

The trip home was euphoric for Ivan. He hadn't realized how much he had missed everyone until the train pulled in at the station in Hitreshety. Vera was there to meet him, and she had never looked so lovely. Ivan was sure she had grown prettier and sweeter and more mature.

And of course she said yes to his proposal. She would become his wife. Ivan went back to the army base with the promise that they would marry in June.

The next few weeks flew by in a flurry of activity for Ivan. He began to wonder if all his worries over becoming an officer were unfounded. The Bible studies with the men were going well—he now met with groups of men nearly every night of the week.

Could it be that like Daniel of old, Ivan was being blessed in spite of the difficult circumstances the devil was throwing his way? Was it a coincidence that his story paralleled the story of Daniel so closely, that their adventures were similar in so many ways?

But would the smooth sailing continue indefinitely? Surely the devil had other plans! Ivan realized that even if God was blessing him in his missionary efforts, the devil still craved a foothold in the lives of the men on the army base. Until now Satan had seen to it that those thousands of soldiers were steeped in darkness and ignorance. They didn't know who Jesus was, let alone what He wanted to do for them as their Savior.

Ivan was sure that sooner or later things would take a turn for the worse. He wasn't by nature a pessimist, but he was a realist. Like Job, it seemed inevitable that Ivan would be called upon to suffer for the sake of Christ! In light of all the blessings he had received, it seemed only fair.

Then Ivan thought of something else. Was it possible that the forces of evil were enticing him away from fulfilling his commission to spread the gospel? Could it be that his acceptance of a promotion as an officer might make him proud or vain and thereby prevent him from reaching the men on the army base? Would his lofty status become a barrier that would jeopardize their chances of receiving the message of salvation?

After that terrifying thought, Ivan began to spend even more time in earnest prayer. He became convinced that he needed to seek a sign from God as to whether or not he should become an officer. Finally he decided that if the military brass continued to woo him as officer material but did not prevent him from giving Bible studies to the soldiers on the base, he would know he was safe. He would know that he was making the right decision in accepting the special favors they were heaping upon him.

However, if they should discontinue his Bible study privileges in any way, then Ivan would know that he had been right all along in resisting their requests that he become an officer.

Ivan continued to visit with the colonel in his office. Often they shared a good laugh over some story the colonel had to tell, or one of Ivan's peculiar habits the colonel had recently discovered. But always the conversations managed to turn to the God of heaven.

One brisk day when Ivan arrived at the colonel's office for his daily work orders, the officer seemed especially somber. Spring was in the air, and the colonel was gazing out his window at the fresh green leaves appearing on the trees all over the military base.

Ivan waited politely at the door until Colonel Ratovsky finally acknowledged his presence. "Come in, my boy. Come in. I sent for you because I have a favor to ask of you, and you were the only one I felt I could really count on just now."

"Anything you ask, sir."

"Thank you, Ivan." It was one of the rare times the colonel addressed Ivan by his first name.

Ivan quickly sent up a prayer for help to meet the challenge at hand—by the look on the colonel's face, this must be a serious moment.

"My mother has died," the colonel began. "It was unexpected. I knew that she had been ill this winter, and I visited her on two different occasions, but I never even saw this coming." The colonel grew quiet again and stared at the rolling hills far beyond the military commons.

"I have always thought of myself as a strong man, Ivan—one who knows his own mind, and one who knows his own heart. I have always felt that when death should come knocking at my door, I would be ready to face it willingly, and even unafraid." He turned in his swivel chair and looked straight at Ivan. "But this unexpected death of one whom I knew so well, and cherished . . ." His voice faltered and caught in his throat before he could go on.

"Would you be willing to go to the funeral with me?" His eyes filled with sorrow as he continued hesitantly. "My father passed on several years ago, and I have no brothers or sisters. I'm the only one left."

"Absolutely," Ivan replied quietly, but said little else. He had learned that at times like this, the less said, the better.

Ivan had been to many funerals, but when the two of them arrived at the residence where the body lay, the scene that greeted them was depressing. So depressing, in fact, that Ivan had to call upon God to help lift his own spirits. It seemed as though the devil were there with all his demon hosts, working to smother any hope of life that remained among the small company gathered for the service.

CHAPTER 19

The house was still and silent, its windows dressed in dark, somber colors. The body of the deceased was shrouded in black, resting in a simple casket of finished pine. It appeared that little had been done to make the colonel's mother appear as she had in life.

They must have rushed the preparations for the funeral, Ivan mused. Her hair had not been done up properly, and the old dress she wore was stained and wrinkled. Evidently the colonel had not had time to meet with the people who were in charge of the burial.

From his conversations with the colonel, Ivan discerned that the old woman had lived a hard life. Born into a poor family of peasants somewhere around the year 1880, she had lived through the final days of the Russian czar, the terror of World War I, and the bloodshed of the Bolshevik Revolution.

Lenin had promised great things for the poor citizens of the newly formed Soviet Union, but then Joseph Stalin had taken the reins of the government. From that day forward the common folks, like Colonel Ratovsky's mother, had learned to fear the dictator more than they feared death itself.

Now the old woman lay awaiting her final resting place, and Ivan thought her face looked peaceful. A faint smile creased the corners of her mouth, as though she were content to be free at last from the hard world into which she had been born.

Ivan listened as a Russian Orthodox priest droned on endlessly, mumbling his incantations as though he himself were preparing for death. No reference was made to Scripture or to the hope of a soon-coming King who would raise her to the bright future of the hereafter.

After what seemed an eternity, the priest finished his eulogy, and an old man came and closed the lid to the coffin. There was a severe note of finality at the sound of the lid dropping into place. The smell of death filled the room, and for a moment Ivan began to feel morose and gloomy. But he took a deep breath and lifted his thoughts heavenward, thanking the Lord that he needn't fear death as most Russians did.

Two old babushkas busied themselves making sure everything was in place. They draped the coffin in greenery, and a black-and-red sash. The coffin was then hoisted to the shoulders of the men selected to transport the body, and a giant wreath was brought out to lead the procession. A motley band with brass instruments arrived at the last minute to accompany the funeral train down the narrow dirt street.

The day was dreary and cloudy, with little to cheer the small group following the casket. Again Ivan felt himself being sucked into the depression of the moment as the funeral train marched slowly to the mournful dirge being played by the brass band. Ivan had been to funerals of this sort before, but most of the deceased he had known were Seventh-day Adventist Christians, and the relatives honored the death of a loved one by focusing on the celebration of the eternal life to come.

Ivan saw that the whole experience was difficult for Colonel Ratovsky. By the time the funeral was over, Ivan wasn't sure he was going to be able to pull the man out of his despondent state.

"Do you mind if I come in?" the colonel sighed when he and Ivan arrived back at Ivan's apartment.

Ivan stoked the coals in his fireplace and then prepared some hot tea for the colonel.

"She was a good woman, and I know that she did not worry about the future," the colonel began. "As you say, your God has a heaven for those who choose to worship Him. I believe that my mother will enjoy such a reward, but—" Here he hesitated with a sigh, as though fearing to finish the thought. It seemed that the death of his mother had brought him face to face with his own uncertain future—as though the fear of death was haunting him from beyond his own grave.

They sat for some time and said nothing. Ivan sensed that the colonel was drawing strength from just being with him. The last thing the man needed right now was a sermon on faith. However, he also knew that the demons of despondency needed to be driven away. It was the only way to help the colonel escape the deep despair that threatened to overwhelm him. What he needed was a friend and a message of genuine hope, but the Holy Spirit would have to take charge if this was going to happen.

"Sir, I am so sad that you have had to suffer such a loss. I cannot imagine what it would be like to lose my mother." Ivan bowed his head in sympathetic grief for this officer he had come to love.

"But your mother was a good woman," Ivan added, "and she loved the Lord. God has her life and her memory in the palm of His hand. Like your mother, we don't need to fear death. We can be sure of eternal life, and one day—like your mother—live in the earth made new."

"I wish I could believe that," the colonel murmured, "but right now I'm not so sure. I always thought I wouldn't be afraid to die, but now this experience has left me wondering what would happen to me if I had to face death today. I mean, I don't even know what death is. How can I be sure of where I'm going if death is such a mystery?"

"Death is a mystery," Ivan agreed, "but Jesus has torn away the darkness and uncertainty of the grave. He died for the sins of the world and forever paid the debt that you and I owe."

Ivan's face lit up with the assurance of hope. "We can thank God that Jesus rose from the grave. He escaped the vicelike grip of death, and because of this, you and I can look forward to the hope of eternal life. His resurrection is proof of that fact."

Ivan went to his bedside and got his Bible. "Death is like a sleep," he said as he turned its pages to some of his favorite passages. "When Jesus' good friend Lazarus died, Jesus said that Lazarus was sleeping the sleep of death. To God, that's what death is like. It doesn't have to be the end of everything for us. When we die, we're just sleeping under His watchcare."

The light of truth danced in Ivan's eyes as he sat down beside the colonel. "The good part about this is that when Jesus comes again, it will be time for the dead to wake up again. Paul, a great writer in the Bible, says that when that great day arrives, the trumpet will sound, and the dead who believed in Jesus will be raised up, never to see death again—and then those of us who have been waiting for our loved ones will be 'caught up together with them in the clouds . . . : and so shall we ever be with the Lord' [1 Thess. 4:17]."

There was a quiet calm in the room as Ivan paused. It was as if all the comfort of heaven had come to rest upon the place.

"So that means that if I believe in God, I don't need to worry about death or the fear of death." The colonel said the words haltingly, as if they were too good to be true.

Ivan laid his hand confidently on the colonel's shoulder. "If you believe in the Lord Jesus Christ, you will be saved."

"I do believe," Colonel Ratovsky replied, bowing his head. "You make it all so clear—I can't help believing. It gives me something to live for." A silent tear trickled down his cheek at the solemn thought. Then he lifted his head and looked out the window. "More important, it gives me something to die for."

It was a day of transformation in the life of the colonel, a day he would remember for the rest of his life.

CHAPTER 20

There were others in the camp whose lives were forever touched by Ivan. Boris, the head cook in the kitchen, became a good friend of Ivan's. He was a short, stocky man with huge forearms and a crooked grin. Unfortunately, he had a bad habit of swearing that nearly curled Ivan's hair.

However, he had taken great pains from the beginning to see that Ivan had all the kinds of food he wanted, and not just because Colonel Ratovsky demanded it. From time to time Ivan had stopped in and offered suggestions as to what the sick men in camp needed to eat in order to get well.

Sometimes Ivan prescribed charcoal as a treatment for stomach dysentery brought on by bad water. The charcoal could be obtained from burned toast or even from scraping the burned food off the bottoms of pans. Ivan also showed Boris how to gather sumac berries and green pine needles to make tea as a tonic for the men who were ailing and short on vitamins.

Ivan was also a positive influence in supplementing his own diet with healthy foods instead of the meats Boris served. Beans and peas helped out a lot and cheese could be gotten sometimes, but eggs were not as common.

But Ivan had never gotten used to Boris's constant swearing, and in the end it was this habit that drew the two men together—not so much because they got along, but because their lifestyles and speaking habits were so different.

When things went wrong in the kitchen, the men eating in the mess hall could hear Boris's profanity loud and clear. The recruits in camp were used to the cursing, but Ivan realized there had to be a reason behind Boris's anger and profanity, especially the words aimed directly at God. This perplexed Ivan, since few Russians in the army claimed to believe in God.

"Why do you swear so much?" Ivan finally asked one day when they were alone in the mess hall kitchen.

The question was blunt, and it took Boris by surprise. Not so much because it was out of character for Ivan to ask it, but because he had the courage to say it. Very few people in camp ever dared to confront Boris like this. They were too dependent on the food he served them and too afraid of what he might put in it if he got angry with them.

Boris laughed uproariously. "So you don't like my swearing!" He picked up a crate of cabbage and carried it to one of the wooden tables sitting in the center of the kitchen. "If I swear, what is it to you? It doesn't make you more evil. I'm the one who is bad."

"Because I know anger when I see it." Ivan began to help Boris unload the crate. "And I know the human heart. You wouldn't swear so much if it weren't for something in your life that made you this angry."

Ivan shrugged. "It can be like that for any of us. Maybe we had a rough time when we were kids, or maybe a girl broke our hearts."

Boris grabbed a big butcher knife and began chopping the cabbage into wedges. But he didn't say anything.

"Maybe you're bitter inside because the pain just won't go away and you're so angry that sometimes you think you're just going to explode."

Boris laid the knife down and stared at the pile of cabbage on the table in front of him.

"God knows about the pain, Boris. He too wishes that the pain would go away. He can't take us out of this world every time things go wrong, but He can give us courage to face the pain and strength to deal with it."

Boris began to scoop up the cabbage and put it in a large kettle sitting on a cart next to the table. "How do you know all this stuff?" he demanded. "I mean, the way you talk about all this stuff, it's like you're a doctor of the mind or something."

Ivan smiled. "I'm no doctor—just a country boy who has found God and knows He's the answer to all the problems in my life. And He can do it for you, too, Boris."

Boris shook his head. "Nobody can fix my life, Gumenyuk! Nobody! It's too messed up!"

"God can do anything, Boris. He can heal the blind. He can make the deaf hear. He can heal lepers, and He can even raise the dead. He wants to give you peace, Boris. Jesus said, 'Come to Me, all you who are burdened and are living under a heavy load of guilt—I can give you rest for your soul' [see Matt. 11:28]."

Boris glared at Ivan impatiently. "So you're telling me your God is interested in me? What have I ever done for Him? Nothing, I tell you. Nothing! All I've ever given Him is rage and enough cusswords to last me an eternity in hell! He wouldn't be interested in me even if He does exist!"

"Who told you about hell? Who told you that God doesn't exist?" Ivan countered.

Boris continued staring at Ivan. "What do you mean, who told me? Everyone told me! They taught us that in school! Didn't your instructors and preceptor teach you that God doesn't exist? Ha! Even the Soviet army tells us that!"

"And do you believe that?" Ivan's voice was quiet but steady.

"I—I don't know what I believe anymore!" Boris bent over the table and struck it with his fist. "I don't know what I believe!" For a long moment the kitchen was silent, except for the sound of the fire crackling in the stove.

Boris finally broke the silence. "When I was a little boy, my grandfather used to tell me about God. He said that God is good and wants to give good things to His children. But then he died. He got something terrible—the doctor didn't know what it was, but it ate him up inside until he wasted away to nothing but skin and bones. And the day they put my grandfather in the ground, I guess I stopped believing in such a thing as God."

Boris had a determined look in his eye, but Ivan only waited.

"Since that day my whole life has fallen apart! I've done a lot of bad things in my life, Gumenyuk! A lot of bad things!" He shook his head emphatically. "You don't want to know about all the bad stuff I've done!"

"That's right, Boris," Ivan finally spoke up. "No one needs to hear about all that bad stuff. Only God needs to know, but He still loves you anyway. You just need to come back to Him and get Him into your life again. That's all."

Boris shook his head. "It's not that easy!"

"It can be that easy," Ivan kept on, "but we need to confess to Him all our wrongs. We need to tell God about all the bad stuff so that we can be free of the guilt and hurting that has filled our lives because of it. That's all we need to do—it's all we *can* do."

Ivan's voice grew quiet. "'If we confess our sins, [God] is faithful and just to forgive us our sins, and . . . [He will] cleanse us from all unrighteousness' [1 John 1:9]."

Boris lifted his head and sighed. "And then what?"

"That's it." Ivan shrugged.

"That's it? Isn't there something I have to do to get saved? Isn't there a paper I've got to buy or something like that to pay for the sins I've done?"

Ivan shook his head.

"It can't be that simple! I've got to do something! I've heard that some people fast, and sometimes people get a priest to pray for their sins!"

Ivan continued shaking his head. "It's already been done, Boris. You don't need to do anything more. Jesus died for you to pay for your sins because He knew you could never make up for all the wrongs you've done. But if you ask Jesus, He can make you clean—whiter than snow, like the Bible says" (see Isa. 1:18).

The look that came over Boris's face at that moment was truly incredible. As long as Ivan lived, he would never see a man more at peace than Boris looked in that instant.

CHAPTER 21

The winter had been long and the training strenuous. As spring arrived, many of the soldiers on the base began to ship out to points unknown. Ivan realized that his days with these men were numbered, and it worried him. Many of them had accepted Jesus as their Savior, but Ivan wanted them to have a chance to be baptized.

There were Viktor and Stefan, two brothers who had arrived at the base just before Ivan. Orphans, they had never really had a place that they could call home. Many times they had reminded Ivan that the day he had arrived on the army base was the best day of their lives. "You are like a father to us," they said. "A spiritual one, at least." And they all laughed, because Viktor was several years older than Ivan.

Mykola was the best marksman in Ivan's original unit. This fact had made it difficult for him ever since he had given his heart to Jesus. In spite of his repeated efforts to obtain conscientious objector status so that he wouldn't have to carry a gun, the sergeant in his platoon wouldn't release him.

"He's too valuable to the unit," the sergeant had said again and again. "He's as good a marksman as anyone I've ever had here on the base."

"But his religious convictions prevent him from using a gun effectively," Ivan had argued. "If you get into a fire exchange, he may end up cracking under the pressure."

"I'll take that chance," the sergeant had insisted.

Petya was a big man—he was the soldier who had challenged Ivan about his vegetarian diet during their first week in boot camp. Petya was more than six feet tall and weighed an even 100 kilos, about 220 pounds. He had been one of the first to begin studying the Bible with Ivan, and what a change had come over him when he gave his heart to Jesus!

And then there was Andryi. He was the most spiritual of all the soldiers in Ivan's study groups. He would be the one most likely to lead out in a new study group wherever he was sent. And right now it was looking more and more as though Viktor and Stefan would be part of that group. Ivan had heard that the two brothers and Andryi were being shipped out together to the Balkans.

And there were others—23 in all. They were an unusual bunch, and Ivan made arrangements for all of them to go home with him and be baptized. This was kept secret, of course, and not all of the men rode together on the same train to the village of Hitreshety. That would certainly have raised the suspicions of their commanding officers.

However, when they arrived in Hitreshety, a new problem posed itself—where and when to have the baptism? At night when the weather was warm, the local police were in the habit of guarding the swimming holes and bends in the river where the church was known to baptize its new members.

But would they be worried about a baptism this time of year? It was early spring, and the days were still chilly yet. Rumors from town said that the police figured it was still early enough in the spring that no one would dare be baptized for fear of catching pneumonia. But Ivan wasn't sure he could trust rumors, so he decided to do the unthinkable, just in case.

On a Sunday afternoon, in broad daylight, when he felt sure the authorities would be the least suspicious, Ivan led all the candidates down to the Prut River—the same place he and his friends from the young people's group had spent so many hours together. He had been careful not to introduce any of the young men to the church members in Hitreshety. That way, if the authorities ever asked questions, no one would know who had been baptized.

The sky was a broad swath of blue satin that spring afternoon. Early returning swallows swooped low to get a look at the unlikely bunch crowding the muddy riverbank. Big fluffy white clouds scudded over the Moldovan landscape as the young soldiers took their baptismal vows and one by one were immersed in the slow-moving waters. It was a weekend none of them would ever forget.

"I salute you battle warriors!" Ivan called out quietly to the men shivering on the banks of the river. "You are now soldiers of the cross of Christ. Never forget that!

"From this day forward you must contend with the evil principalities of this world, the rulers of darkness, the spiritual hosts of wickedness in high places who will stop at nothing in order to see you all fail in your mission." Ivan was emphatic.

"And so I challenge you today to put on the whole armor of God so that you can stand before the attacks of the devil. Take with you God's truth as it has been taught to you," Ivan commanded. "Put on the breastplate of Christ's righteousness, the shield of faith, the helmet of salvation, and the sword of His Spirit. And everywhere you go, take with you the Word of God (see Eph. 6:10-20). With it and the rest of God's armor, you will quench all the fiery darts of the devil and his demon hosts.

"My heart goes with you, men!" There were tears in Ivan's voice. "Some of you will suffer for God, and some of you may die before you return home! But don't be afraid! Endure the hardships you receive as soldiers of the cross, and in the end, when Jesus comes again, you will receive a crown of life!"

Each man was given a small Bible, and then Ivan quietly led them in a hymn he had taught them at the Bible studies in the barracks: "Onward Christian soldiers marching as to war, with the cross of Jesus going on before! Christ our royal master leads against the foe, forward into battle, see His banners go!"

The men grew more animated in their singing, and Ivan had to quiet them down as they sang the chorus of the hymn triumphantly. "Onward, Christian soldiers! marching as to war, with the cross of Jesus going on before!"

That was the last time the men were all together. Ivan knew he would never forget the bravery of these men, the first of his converts in the Soviet army.

But as these men began to ship out from the army base, one by one others came to take their place in the Bible study groups. Ivan understood, of course, that future converts would also leave him after their training was over. The base was designed to be a boot camp, a place the soldiers remained six months at the most. That's all Ivan could expect.

This realization caused him many sleepless nights, and with renewed energy and prayer he doubled his efforts for the salvation of these men.

Ivan was married a short time later on a balmy day in early June. The ceremony was a small one, since Soviet law forbade holding weddings in a typical church setting. There wasn't much space in the front room of Vera's childhood home, but family, friends, and church members spilled out into the front yard, peering in the windows to get a glimpse of the happy couple.

Ivan could hardly believe this day had finally arrived. He loved this young woman, and together they would meet the uncertain but exciting future. Important days lay ahead for Ivan, but with Vera by his side, he felt he could face anything.

CHAPTER 22

Ivan had almost forgotten how much he missed Vera, how soft her hands were, and how good her sweet smile made him feel. At times the true love they shared thrilled Ivan's heart to overflowing. Without a doubt it was a marriage made in heaven.

The happy couple settled right in at Ivan's apartment. In no time at all Vera had the few dishes and linens out of their crates and into the cupboards prepared for them. And of course she added a feminine touch to the apartment, as only a woman can do. Curtains in the kitchen window, flowers in a vase on the reading table, a freshly made bed—all told of her love for this young man who was becoming such an important figure on the army base.

Vera loved keeping house for Ivan. Every morning he would leave to work with the colonel on the day's administrative assignments. Each evening he would come home to a warm-cooked meal prepared by his young bride. Like her mother, Vera was an excellent cook. Her tasty food soon became the envy of the army base, since Ivan would often invite young soldiers home for a meal. Colonel Ratovsky occasionally came by to sample her delicious spice cake, and even Boris appeared on the doorstep to gather a few tips from Vera.

For a while it appeared as though Colonel Ratovsky and General Shevchenko had forgotten their wishes to advance Ivan on through the officers' ranks—but Ivan knew it would be only a matter of time before they'd begin pressuring him again.

A few weeks after Vera's arrival at the base, Ivan came home one evening to find her holding an invitation to another one of the elite banquets for high-ranking army officials. When she handed him the gold-embossed invitation printed on official army stationery, he knew they were at it again.

"These rascals are cagey," Ivan laughed. "Now they want you to come too, Vera. They know exactly what they're doing, don't they?"

Three days before the big event, a sergeant came by to deliver two gift-wrapped boxes for Vera. In one she found a beautiful blue satin evening gown. In the other was a jeweled necklace studded with a score of diamonds, which she knew must be worth more money than she could ever imagine.

When Ivan came home, she handed him the necklace. He simply shook his head when he saw the glittering piece. "They'll stop at nothing," he murmured. "I guess they don't know you, do they, dear? How could they know that you've never worn a stitch of jewelry in your life?"

Ivan could tell Vera was upset about the gifts. Probably not so much because of the temptation it represented, but because she was worried that she might somehow become a pawn in this game for Ivan's future.

It was a serious game, though, and she wanted nothing to do with it. "We need to give the necklace back," she finally said.

"You can do as you wish," Ivan assured her, "but they'll probably just try to give you bigger and more expensive gifts—maybe not always jewelry, but gifts to entice you just the same."

Vera put the necklace away in a safe place, but went dressed in the evening gown they had provided for her.

When their chauffeur pulled up to the location of the evening affair, a plain-looking warehouse greeted them. Vera glanced up and down the street, and then again at the warehouse.

"Where are they taking us?" she asked, perplexed. "This must be the wrong address." The building certainly didn't appear to be a place that high-ranking military personnel and officers would hold a political rally or banquet. However, Ivan assured her that soon she would see the place for what it really was.

A uniformed military guard opened the car door for them and escorted the young couple to the entrance. Inside they were led down a dim corridor and then into an elaborately furnished hall that was clearly out of touch with the rest of Soviet society. Quite appropriately, the extravagance of exclusive military occasions was disguised.

Immediately in front of them the military personnel mingled in a large, luxurious chamber with ornate Persian rugs elegantly arranged on the floor. To the left was another large chamber with polished oak flooring ready for ballroom dancing and dining. Sparkling chandeliers hung in profusion from the ceilings, and a small orchestra in one corner was playing well-known pieces from Tchaikovsky and Stravinsky. Everywhere they looked they saw opulence and elegance fit for royalty.

Sumptuous food awaited the palate of anyone who loved fine cuisine. There was salmon and cracked crab all the way from the coast and, of course, the usual caviar and fine wines.

Vera had never been to a lavish banquet before, but if Ivan thought she would be out of place, he was wrong. She appeared most enchanting in her blue satin gown, and throughout the entire evening she was surrounded by a group of interested bystanders who appreciated her wit and charm.

Colonel Ratovsky leaned toward Ivan on one occasion and furtively whispered, "Your wife is not wearing the jewelry we sent. Does she not like it? We can exchange it for something else, if she prefers."

Ivan gave the colonel a knowing glance. "You'll have to ask her about that yourself."

For Ivan the evening was a continual round of introductions as usual. He had met many of the high-ranking officials previously, but there were some new faces. General Shevchenko introduced Ivan to Secretary Antonovich, a member of the Kremlin's politburo.

"So this is Gumenyuk?" The bald man gazing over the top of his spectacles was as imposing as his gray-blue uniform had been designed for him to appear. "I understand they're making a first-rate officer out of you," he added with a click of his heals.

"They're trying, sir." In spite of his facade, Ivan thought the secretary had a winsome way about him.

"What are you now, son? A lieutenant?"

Colonel Ratovsky leaned toward the secretary. "He'll be a captain in a matter of weeks, sir. This young man has risen through the ranks more quickly than any officer I've ever trained before. He just has too much raw talent to waste on anything less than the rank of captain."

Antonovich nodded. "Excellent! Where's your home, son? What does your father do?" Ivan felt the secretary's eyes scrutinizing him.

"I come from the village of Hitreshety, sir. It's about 100 kilometers from here—my father is a farmer."

"A farmer, is he? H'mmm—and what do you hope to make of yourself? Are you going to become a career officer?"

This was the question that could potentially bring him trouble every time it was asked, and especially when it came from a government official from Moscow. And yet it had to be answered. There was no doubt in Ivan's mind now that he was being set in high places for just such a time as this. God's name was to be lifted to its proper place, and Ivan was the one to do it.

"I wish to be a missionary for God, sir." Ivan's intense blue eyes looked straight into the secretary's.

The officers standing near Ivan suddenly grew quiet, and the effect rippled across the banquet hall until the entire room took on an unearthly silence.

"A missionary!" The secretary appeared confused. "A missionary—to do—what?"

"I wish to tell others of the goodness of God."

"H'mmm." The secretary considered the thought for a moment. "A missionary." He searched Ivan's face for telltale signs that they were really having this conversation, and that it wasn't some kind of gag set up by one of the other officers.

But Ivan returned the secretary's searching gaze unashamedly. He could feel the Holy Spirit giving him courage once again to stand as a witness for God—even with this influential member of the highest-ranking government office in the Soviet Union.

"It must be that the military has not been treating you right, son." The secretary looked perplexed. "Why else would you choose to abandon your responsibilities here? Why leave the opportunity of a lifetime?"

All eyes were on Ivan now. He knew that he and his God were on display. His response could make or break any opportunities he might have in the future to be a beacon of truth on the army base. So many soldiers had learned so much from the Bible studies he had been holding during the previous year—Ivan couldn't let those men down now, and he couldn't let God down.

"God has called me to be His witness, sir. Wherever I go, I must speak boldly for Him. You see, Jesus, God's Son, came to this earth and became a man to die for me. If it wasn't for my sins, He wouldn't have had to do that, but I'm so glad that He did."

Ivan grinned boyishly. "And now, sir, I can't help telling everyone the good news. It's like fire in my veins, and I must share it with anyone who will listen. Right now I'm in the military, so for the time being, I'll be God's missionary here."

Ivan paused to let his words find their mark before continuing. He felt calm and collected—his pulse was steady, and his breathing was even. This was yet another classic moment when he felt that time stood still, but what happened next nearly took his breath away.

"So—did this Jesus die for me, too?"

Someone, somewhere in the room, gasped, and then absolute silence again gripped the vast chamber. The secretary's question had taken even Ivan by surprise.

Was the secretary serious? Did he really want an answer to his question, or was he simply mocking Ivan for the naïveté of his Christian beliefs? Instantly Ivan decided that the secretary was probably searching for truth.

"Jesus died for you, Secretary Antonovich. You are precious in His sight. Your sins before God are many, but if you will ask Him to forgive you for the wrongs you have done, He will cleanse you and make you right before God."

Several guests near Ivan caught their breath. How could this mere lieutenant say such things to a high-ranking Soviet official? Surely the wrath of Moscow would now descend upon the young man with all its force!

But Ivan wasn't finished. Glancing around the plush ballroom, he addressed the speechless guests. "Jesus died for every person in this room, and any day now He will return in the clouds of heaven to give everyone their reward—those of us who have accepted His offer of eternal life, as well as those of us who have rejected it."

The words were solemn, and they found their mark. Before long the party broke up, and everyone headed home.

On their way home in the car that night, Vera snuggled close to Ivan. She was so proud of her husband. Not just because he had been the center of attention that evening, but because he was so close to God that the Holy Spirit could speak through him and present salvation to a room full of Communist government leaders.

CHAPTER 23

Two days later Ivan was in Colonel Ratovsky's office late in the afternoon. A warm breeze drifted in through the open window, and katydids hummed in the oak trees outside. It had been a quiet, lazy day. Several regiments of troops had just been shipped out to distant posts of duty, so there wasn't much going on at the base.

"Thank you for stopping by." The colonel offered Ivan a chair.

"Gumenyuk, when my mother died, you helped me believe that there is a life after death. You helped me believe in a God, and you gave me hope. It all sounded so simple, so easy." The colonel paused, and his face grew troubled.

"And then I listened as you spoke the other night at the evening ball." Colonel Ratovsky squinted at Ivan through the shafts of afternoon sunlight slanting in through the window. "I've been thinking about what you said to Secretary Antonovich—that one day Jesus is coming to reward everyone for the lives they have led."

The colonel sighed and then continued. "I have not led a good life, Gumenyuk. I am a hard man. I have spent my entire adult life working in the military and did not get where I am by being nice."

Ivan knew that what Colonel Ratovsky said was probably true. Military officers were especially known for their meanness of spirit and characteristic brutality. Their reputations were second only to that of the KGB.

"I know we've had these discussions before," the colonel added, "but somehow, that night there in the room with all those high-ranking officials, you said it even better. I felt something tugging on my heart—both the desire to take what God has to offer and the fear that I must one day pay for all the horrible wrongs I have done."

Ivan saw discouragement written on the colonel's face. He

106

looked almost as downhearted as he had when his mother died.

Ivan had to say something. There was no other option.

"God wants better things for you, Colonel. His Holy Spirit is speaking to your heart now. He knows the struggles you face here on the base and the ones you have battled in your personal life. He knows all the terrible things you have done."

"So, what do I have to do, Ivan? I do believe in God, and that's just the problem. I don't want to face a judgment before Him. I want the reward of eternal life you talked about."

"Then you must give your heart and your life to God again. Every day you must do this. Every day of your life you must surrender all your fears to Him. It's the only way. It's what I have to do every day myself," Ivan added.

The colonel shook his head at Ivan. "For you it may be easy, but for me it's against my nature. Believe me! I've tried! I've thought about it many a night! Sometimes I think I want God to be a part of my life, and sometimes I don't! It's like a battle raging inside of me!"

Ivan looked intently at the colonel, and he knew that what the man said was true—there was a struggle going on inside of him. There were unseen forces at work here. "This kind of surrender doesn't bring victory, except through much prayer." Ivan uttered the words solemnly, as though he were taking a sentence right out of the Gospels.

"What do you mean by that?" The colonel nervously studied Ivan's face.

"You are not wrestling with flesh and blood, Colonel, but with the forces and rulers of spiritual darkness, against the hosts of evil in high places. They are competing for your soul, and they don't want to give you up to God without a fight. The heart of every human is a battleground for the forces of good and evil," Ivan added earnestly.

A look of fear crept across the colonel's face. "Rulers of darkness? Are you talking about demons and devils?"

"Exactly." Ivan pulled his chair close to the colonel's desk. "The devil—or Satan, as some call him—has been after you your whole life so that he can steal your soul and rob you of eternal life."

"But I always thought that the devil was a mythological character! I didn't think he was real." The colonel's voice began to tremble.

"That's exactly what he wants you to think. If he can get you to believe that he is make-believe, then he doesn't have to work as hard. But in the end he will still get your soul."

"W—well, what do I need to do to shake this thing? Won't God help me? I thought you said your God wants to save me."

"He does, but you must believe. All your life you never believed in the devil, but you never believed in God or His power, either. Today you must make a choice, Colonel. God wants to help you, but you must step out in faith and believe that He can and will."

"I want to believe." The officer leaned across his large mahogany desk, a desperate plea in his eyes. "Help me to believe, Ivan!" It wrung Ivan's heart to hear the powerful officer begging for help.

It had been a warm afternoon, and Ivan had wiped sweat from his forehead several times during their conversation—but now he felt the air grow chilly around him. He sensed a strange presence in the room, and he knew exactly what was happening. Satan was marshaling his forces to fight for and hang on to what he felt was rightfully his.

But the battle for every soul belongs to God, and Ivan wanted to be sure that this battle for the colonel's soul wouldn't be in vain. Leaning over to the bookshelf, Ivan took down the Bible he had given the colonel as a gift and turned its pages to certain passages.

Reading aloud those Bible texts, Ivan warned the colonel that the devil was stalking him like a hungry lion, and that he needed to put on the whole armor of God. He needed the shield of faith so that he could quench all the fiery darts of the devil. If the colonel would resist the devil with the help of God's power, then the devil would flee.

The two men knelt in prayer, and Ivan prayed fervently for this Russian officer who had denied God's existence all his life but was now ready to face the truth. He was now ready to believe and to let the power of God work in his life.

Gradually the room began to warm again—it appeared that the moment of crisis had passed. The battle for the colonel's heart had been won, at least for the time being.

"That was the strangest experience I've ever had," the colonel confessed as they got up from their knees. "What just happened here?"

Ivan looked at the colonel—the officer obviously still had much to learn. "Well, sir, you just experienced the first major battle between good and evil for your soul. We Christians call it the great controversy between Christ and Satan, and that's exactly what it is. This controversy has been raging for thousands of years over who is right and who will win in the end—God or Satan."

"So is the battle over? Did I win?"

"You won that battle, but there will be many more to come," Ivan promised.

And so it went as Ivan taught the colonel how to live a victorious life. In spiritual things Ivan was the master teacher and Colonel Ratovsky the pupil.

In October Ivan and Vera were invited to a political rally in Kiev hosted by the Kremlin. The missing jeweled necklace and Vera's reasons for not wearing it were not discussed again. But this time a tissue-wrapped box for Vera showed up at their apartment with a fox fur in it. The sheen of the silver fur glistened as Vera took it out of the box, and again it seemed too extravagant a gift for her modest Christian tastes.

Vera decided to take the fur with them on their train trip to the capital of the Ukraine, but not because the evenings were turning cooler or because she admired the stole. "I want Colonel Ratovsky to know we appreciate all he's doing for us," she confided to Ivan. "If I wear the fur, do you think it will put more pressure on you to become a full-fledged officer?" Ivan could tell that this was a struggle for her. The last thing she wanted was to hinder Ivan's opportunities to witness for God.

The trip to Kiev was a wonderful experience for both Ivan and Vera, and again Ivan got pushed to the forefront at the rally—this time in a very political way. The rally was no mere evening dance. It was three days of speeches and parades that were designed to bolster Ukraine support for the latest political ventures of the Kremlin. Ivan was introduced to so many officials and figureheads that he despaired of ever being able to remember them all.

"Don't worry about that," Colonel Ratovsky remarked once. "Sometimes I forget their names too." He smiled sheepishly. "If they are a superior officer, I just call them 'sir.' And if I feel it's really important, I ask the doorman who they are."

During the evenings in Kiev, Ivan and Vera were escorted to functions that were less political in nature, but still very formal. Again the evening banquets and ballroom waltzes were held in nonconspicuous places where they would not attract public attention. Ivan began to realize that the average Soviet citizen knew nothing of the comfortable lifestyle military and government officers secretly enjoyed. It seemed so wrong, yet he knew there was nothing he could do about it.

The young couple never did become totally adjusted or comfortable with the evening festivities that were planned at these functions. They usually found good food to eat, but the dances were not something they enjoyed. As Christians they had not been raised dancing, and because of this they always felt very much out of place. They were convinced that those who are preparing for the soon coming of Jesus should concern themselves with more important things than dancing in circles on a ballroom floor.

Back at the army base life returned to normal for Ivan and Vera. Everything seemed to be going well until Colonel Ratovsky called Ivan to his office one day. Ivan now had an office of his own down the hall from the colonel, so it was much easier for them to get together. However, on this occasion Ivan sensed that something was wrong.

"They're going to take you away from me, Ivan." Colonel Ratovsky sat staring at Ivan in disbelief, as though he had just been told that he was terminally ill with cancer.

Ivan stared at the colonel for several moments and then shook his head dizzily. "They're going to do what?" he finally stammered.

"They're transferring you to the army base at Kotovsk. You'll be working for the military Shtab and the administrative offices that report directly to headquarters in Moscow." Colonel Ratovsky shook his head angrily. "This is all Secretary Antonovich's doing!" he added with a wave of his hand, as though he had already resigned himself to Ivan's fate. "I should have known it would happen. I could tell that he liked you the night he met you at the officers' ball."

"They're going to take me away?" Ivan's blue eyes blazed. "They can't take me away! I live here!"

"They can take you, and they will." Colonel Ratovsky's eyes were sad. "I guess we showed you off a little bit too much at all those political rallies."

Ivan bowed his head silently, not knowing what to say. Life would definitely be different now. He began to think of all the changes that would take place in his and Vera's life—and the changes that would come to Colonel Ratovsky's life.

The young lieutenant finally raised his head. "If this comes to pass, it must be the Lord's doing. He has never led me to places that I could not serve Him better."

The colonel nodded his head slowly. "I know you are right, my boy, but it doesn't make the parting any easier. You have been a strength to me for almost a year now, but I will always remember the times we spent together. You have helped make me a better man."

"The Lord is good. He has allowed me to spend many months with you." Ivan's voice was strong, but his eyes began to mist over. "You are like a father to me, and I'm so glad we had this friendship."

They parted a few weeks later, but it was with hope in their hearts and a promise that they would get together as often as their duties allowed them.

CHAPTER 24

Within three weeks Ivan had been transferred to his new position at a military base in Kotovsk. And just as Colonel Ratovsky had guessed, Secretary Antonovich had secured Ivan's transfer. Ivan was now an assistant to another high-ranking officer, which gave him a variety of responsibilities.

Ivan settled in easily and was soon familiar with most of the men on the base. As before, Vera's cooking was popular with the officers, and they often found excuses to come by Ivan's apartment at mealtime. Without fail they were invited in, as though the whole event had been planned.

The officers Ivan now worked with at Kotovsk were very intelligent, and many of them were well educated. They knew a great deal about politics and were always asking for Ivan's opinion on government matters. Ivan would comment from time to time, and he usually added some interesting ideas from the Bible.

When some of the officers invited Ivan to join a regular late-night discussion in the apartment of one of the officers, Ivan accepted the invitation. The meetings were held in a different officer's quarters each time. Always the air was blue with tobacco smoke, and the smell of vodka permeated the room.

Eventually it was Ivan's turn to host the meeting, and he asked Vera to serve them some of her delicious borsch and homemade Russian bread. They knew that Ivan neither smoked nor drank, but no one seemed to mind the missing cigarettes and vodka.

Because many of the officers were avid history buffs, Ivan wisely chose chapter 2 of the book of Daniel for the topic of their discussion that night. He felt this would be a good place to start, because its prophecies dealt with the history of such world nations as Babylon, Greece, and Rome, subjects the men often discussed.

However, the men were surprised at Ivan's use of the Bible as a source of history. They were not familiar with it, of course, and asked him to read the chapter to them. Ivan had only one Bible, the copy he had smuggled in when he first joined the army. It was a relief not to have to keep it hidden now, at least when he was studying with the men in their evening discussions.

Ivan read the chapter and began to explain what the prophet was saying. When he made the comment that Hitler's Third Reich had been destined to fail because the Bible said so in the book of Daniel, the officers became especially excited.

"Do you mean to say that the Bible predicted Germany's fall?" asked one officer.

"The Bible doesn't mention Germany by name, but it does say that after the Roman Empire fell, no empire or nation would ever be strong enough to rule the entire earth." Ivan held up his Bible. "It's all right here in the dream King Nebuchadnezzar had one night.

"Daniel says that the image had feet of iron mixed with clay," Ivan continued. "But as iron doesn't mix with clay, so the nations from that time period forward would be divided. No matter how hard kings and emperors would try, nations would not be powerful enough or influential enough to keep countries cemented together in one world empire."

"That's absurd!" protested one of the younger officers. "We all know that the Soviet Union is becoming a major world power. Eventually Marxist philosophy will dominate the earth."

Ivan was firm. "Not according to the Bible. The prophecies of Daniel are accurate in every detail and have never been proved wrong."

The late-night meetings were a pleasant pastime for the officers, and every evening the number of men grew. Often the officers would ask Ivan to lead out, something he always accepted with a smile. Ivan's knowledge of history and the Bible were truly amazing, and always he found ways to slip the truths of the Bible into their discussions.

Many of the officers began to seek Ivan out to discuss personal issues with him. Often it was late at night before Ivan would finally get to sleep, but he always had an encouraging word for the officers and ended their quiet talks with prayer.

By now Ivan was a favorite with the high-ranking officers on the base, and he was again asked to attend special military functions. Repeatedly his superiors urged him to become a fully decorated officer, with the promise of even further promotions, but always he replied that he was content to remain at a lower rank and work directly with the soldiers—that his one wish was to be a missionary for God.

As before, the officers tried influencing Vera by giving her even more expensive gifts, and whenever possible she graciously declined these gifts. Again Ivan was given his own car and a chauffer to take him wherever and whenever he wanted to go. Ivan came and went as he pleased, and no one questioned him about his status.

Ivan's influence began to grow on the army base in other ways. Because he was honest and trustworthy, and because he was efficient in the way he managed those who worked under him, he was soon asked to take on additional responsibilities.

One such responsibility gave him the title of security deputy for a large warehouse that housed all types of specialty items, such as fine wines, caviar, fur coats, and even imported cars. Only high-ranking army officers and the KGB had access to warehouses like this, so it was considered a real honor to be given such an important responsibility.

His new position at the warehouse gave Ivan a chance to meet people on all levels in the chain of command. Sometimes he was even asked to work after hours to serve the KGB officers who usually came into the warehouse under cover of night.

Being around these powerful men was a bit unnerving for Ivan at first, because he recognized that such men had almost unlimited power and influence in the underworld of Soviet politics. However, Ivan came to realize that these men put their trousers on just the same as ordinary men in the army. And besides, with God at his side, was there really anything for Ivan to worry about?

But the biggest problem associated with his job at the warehouse still loomed on the horizon. Would the Sabbath become an issue? The warehouse was open seven days a week, and therefore he was required to be on the premises to supply the officers with whatever they had requisitioned.

What was he to do? Should he ask someone else to take over the responsibilities for the day? Was he even allowed to do this? Should he just not show up for work? The duty was his, and attention would certainly come his way if he failed to show up.

During the first week of boot camp at Fastof Ivan had been blessed when he took a bold stand on Sabbath observance, but would things go as smoothly here in Kotovsk as they had with Colonel Ratovsky? Should he try something as daring as he had at Fastof? Since Ivan was an officer, he doubted he would have much trouble, but the more he thought about the issue, the more he realized that this might be a test of another nature.

Ivan decided to attend to the prickly business of Sabbath observance right away. On Wednesday of his first week at the warehouse, he began to fast and pray. He prayed that God would not only help him to find a way to solve the problem, but that it would be done in a way that would honor God's holy day and again draw attention to the God of the Bible.

Fasting for three days wasn't impossible—Ivan had fasted longer than that before. He was grateful that he wasn't in training camp, though—it would have been even more difficult.

Vera decided to fast with Ivan. Although they both missed Vera's splendid cooking, they enjoyed the time they spent in praying and studying their Bibles together, and were drawn closer to each other by the experience.

On Thursday evening Ivan stayed awake all night to pray, and by Friday morning he knew what he must do. He would close the warehouse—no one would manage the office.

Friday afternoon, as the sun neared the western horizon, Ivan called the supply sergeant to his office. "We'll be closing up a bit early today," he announced, "and I'll not be coming in tomorrow, either. It's time for the Sabbath."

"Yes, sir," the sergeant saluted respectfully, but after a moment he got a perplexed look on his face. "Sabbath, sir?"

"That's right, Sergeant. Tomorrow is God's holy Sabbath day. It is a day we worship the God of heaven to celebrate His creation of this world."

The sergeant dared to look Ivan in the eye. "Sir?"

"Sergeant," Ivan added, "I'm going to give you the day off tomorrow, but I want you to go to your quarters and rest."

There was another moment's hesitation, and then the sergeant saluted again with a big grin. "Yes, sir!"

A sign was put up announcing that in the future the warehouse would be closed Saturdays and that if anyone needed something during those hours, they were to report back to the office on Sunday morning.

And it worked. That first Sabbath no one of prominence came to the warehouse, and the following Sabbath it was the same. It was as though a subliminal message had gone out to all who had warehouse privileges that Saturdays were no longer days to do business. From that day forward, if anyone needed something, they were to check in at the warehouse well before sundown on Friday.

"Why?" they would inevitably ask.

"Because tomorrow is the Sabbath," they were told, and not always by Ivan, either. The other officers who worked with him had come to know and appreciate the term.

Since visiting the warehouse was a special privilege for a comparative few, most officers probably assumed that the order to close down the warehouse on Saturdays was a command from higher up—which it was, of course. Ivan and Vera knew what that source was, and in the privacy of their little apartment they thanked God for intervening once again in a powerful way.

And all this had happened by the time Ivan was only 21. How a mere boy could have such an impact on the minds and lives of so many was a mystery. It was obvious to Ivan, though, that God was the one working above and behind the scenes to make it all happen.

Like the biblical Daniel, Ivan had decided early on that he would stand for the Christian principles he had been raised with, no matter what the consequences. And because of this, God was able to use him in high places. Because of Ivan's faithfulness, God could trust him with the responsibility of witnessing to the influential men in Soviet uniforms, men who worked with the most powerful leaders of the land.

Often Ivan thought of the quote he had read many times in a book his father kept hidden at home. At this point in his life the words seemed especially appropriate.

"The greatest want of the world is the want of men—men who will not be bought or sold, men who in their inmost souls are true and honest, men who do not fear to call sin by its right name, men whose conscience is as true to duty as the needle to the pole, men who will stand for the right though the heavens fall" (Ellen G. White, *Education*, p. 57).

CHAPTER 25

As the weeks and months passed, Ivan couldn't help wondering how Colonel Ratovsky was doing back at the army base in Fastof. Was he struggling with his newfound faith? Was he having difficulty battling with the demons of vodka and cigarettes? Ivan prayed for him daily, and several times he wrote the colonel letters of encouragement. But the colonel wasn't the letter-writing type, so Ivan longed for the day he could go back to Fastof to visit.

At last the opportunity came. Ivan had put in for a 10-day leave so that he could go home to Hitreshety to visit his family and the church. On the way, he planned to stop by the army base to see Colonel Ratovsky.

When Ivan arrived at the army base, Colonel Ratovsky grabbed Ivan in a bear hug, and then sat him down to have a cup of tea. There was so much catching up to do.

"When you first came to me, I would have offered you a glass of vodka," the colonel laughed, "and I guess I did a time or two. But that's all changed now," he added. "Not that the old temptations don't come knocking at the door."

"You never answered any of my letters," Ivan reminded the colonel.

"And I must apologize for that," the colonel shrugged sheepishly. "But your letters did encourage me, and it was the letters that kept me from giving up several times. Since you left, I haven't had a drop of alcohol, even when the officers get together. They've begun calling me your sidekick." The colonel laughed jovially.

"Imagine that! In the old days I always thought of you as being my sidekick, but now I don't mind the tables turning one bit. You taught me so much about self-control and how the power of God can work in my life. You were right, Ivan," the colonel beamed. "I don't have to struggle with guilt and sin. Jesus took care of that for me at the cross of Calvary." There were tears in the colonel's eyes. "Thank you for introducing me to God, Ivan! I will never be able to repay you for what you did for me!"

Ivan sat listening, too stunned to say much of anything. When he had first arrived at the army base in Fastof, he never would have dreamed that his witness for God could have such a long-lasting and powerful effect on the lives of the people he met. But of course he understood that it wasn't really any of his doing. His words had had an impact, but the source of power had been the Holy Spirit. Ivan smiled contentedly as he listened to the colonel share his testimony. Through the love of Jesus a most unlikely soul had been won for the kingdom of God.

The two men visited all that day and on into the night. The colonel told of the influence he was now having on the men at the base. "I've stopped drinking and smoking, and I don't cuss anymore," the colonel confessed. "I haven't begun keeping the Sabbath yet, but that's next."

Ivan was quick to note that the colonel was now the one making a spiritual impact in the lives of the soldiers and told him so. "I thank God every day for you, Colonel. But now it's your turn to step up to the call of God. It's your turn to teach the men from the Holy Bible as you have been taught. God has chosen you to be a witness for Him.

"You were wise, Colonel, to choose God as your strength when you needed Him most, and because of this you are going to shine like a light on a hill. Until Jesus comes, you will lead many to righteousness, and as your reward you will shine like the stars for ever and ever."

The experience of coming back to find that the colonel had remained faithful to God was encouraging to Ivan, and a new idea began to form in his heart. He would use his position of influence in the military to establish Bible study groups on many of the army bases in Moldova, and possibly even in the Ukraine. He would guide Soviet soldiers to Jesus, train them in the art of giving Bible studies, and then commission them to be witnesses for God in the army.

And so a new form of evangelism was born in the Soviet Union— although Ivan had already begun putting the plan into action. Ivan's first group of recruits at the army base in Fastof had been baptized and sent out to bases in the Balkan region, to Kazakhstan, and even to Moscow. Now he determined to devote his remaining years in the military to do even more—he would build an army within an army.

Two of his recruits, the brothers Viktor and Stefan, wrote to Ivan telling of the success they were having in bringing the gospel to the Russian soldiers in the Balkans. Sometimes the brothers suffered for it, but "the pain and hardship was worth it," said Viktor. Both of the boys were medics, and on one occasion they refused to take part in target practice at the firing range, so a sergeant ordered them to be locked in the stockade for several days.

But in the end they were respected and admired for their unwavering stand. Not only were they honest in every duty and loyal in their support of superior officers—they were also the best medics in the whole regiment.

One letter from the brothers brought word that Petya had been shot by a sniper while on patrol. He had lived for a few hours, but by the time the medics could give him proper medical attention, he had lost too much blood. "But he said to tell you, Lieutenant Gumenyuk, that he will meet you on the other side. He wanted you to know that when Jesus comes again, you will have a star in your crown for bringing him to Jesus." Ivan blinked back tears at the bittersweet news.

"And Petya was such a strong influence in our regiment here in the Balkans," the letter continued. "Before he died, Petya himself brought many other soldiers to Jesus. The seed has been sown, and as you have reminded us so many times, 'the blood of the martyrs is the seed of the church.' Praise God!"

Tears filled Ivan's eyes again and again as he read the letters from the men he had sent out to be soldiers for Christ.

When Ivan returned from his 10-day leave, he decided to put his plan of evangelism into action. Every Sabbath he began going to the army bases at which Adventist boys served and to the bases to which his recent Bible study recruits had already been sent. He spoke with the boys and encouraged them to be true to their principles and strong in the strength that only God can supply.

He related his own simple story of success—how it all started back in Hitreshety when he exercised and studied with the young people down by the river. He told them how uncertain he had been when he first arrived in the army, and how he had promised to be faithful to God and true to the principles he had been taught.

"The Sabbath is so important," Ivan reminded them, "but so is your diet. And even your unwillingness to carry a gun will tell everyone what kind of men you really are.

"And when you don't smoke and drink, your superior officers will come to respect and admire you for your clean lifestyle." Ivan smiled. "Just look at the life of Daniel. He's a perfect example of what God will do for anyone who steps out in faith and lives a righteous life."

Ivan looked at them fondly. "And remember, whatever Jesus asks us to do, He has already done Himself. He never promised us the way would be easy, but He did promise to be with us until the end of the world.

"And boys," he always added, "be faithful to God, even if it should cost you your life. In the end you'll receive a crown of righteousness." Ivan always said these words boldly, but he often had to fight tears at this part.

The young army recruits were amazed at Ivan's testimony, and many decided to follow his leading. It cheered his heart to see these boys being raised up to carry on the larger work of bringing the gospel to the Soviet army.

CHAPTER 26

After five years in the military Ivan decided to return to civilian life. He had faced many hardships and rewarding challenges in the army, but his parents were getting on in years, and he felt the need to care for them now. Besides, he and Vera thought it was about time to start a family.

But above all, Ivan felt impressed that the Lord was calling him to something of even greater importance. As much good as he had accomplished in the army, he could not avoid the almost-overwhelming feeling that God had bigger plans for him as a civilian. He would continue to build a band of witnesses for God's army within the Soviet army, but he would do it from the outside. His task would be to work tirelessly to develop this corps of missionaries in the military, men who would make it their business to witness for Jesus in the army. Like the Waldenses of long ago who sent out their young people to be missionaries, Ivan's recruits were to bring the precious gems of truth to military men in spiritual darkness.

To find the best young recruits for his army corps of missionaries, Ivan had to travel extensively. Hundreds of these boys could be found, but in churches scattered throughout the countries of Moldova and the Ukraine. Most weekends were spent away from home, but Ivan and Vera never complained, though they were often away from each other.

Sometimes Ivan went by train, sometimes by car. Often he had to travel at night, through rain or snow, and always it seemed that he had to labor under a mantle of hardship. Not only did he have to work in secret to avoid the police and the KGB—he had to work for little or no pay.

"I don't care about the money," Ivan often told Vera. "We'll get along. Our bread and water shall be sure—we've been promised that much, and we need little else. After all, who can put a price on a soul? Our only concern now is getting these boys ready to stand for Jesus in the army."

But the devil was not happy with Ivan's latest venture, and set out to stop him. One particular Friday afternoon Ivan left on a trip for one of his training sessions with the young men. A friend, Pastor Stefan, had agreed to take Ivan there in his car, and they were making good progress until they came to a rather muddy patch of road. The winter snows had melted, but the ground was still frozen. This made them feel as though the car was slipping and sliding around on a layer of grease.

The road ran through a hilly part of the landscape with a sharply sloping bank falling away on one side of the road. As they came to a sharp bend in the road, the car began to slide sideways. The pastor tried to regain control of the car, but it was no use. Ivan sat, horrified, in the back seat as the car skidded to the edge of the road and then plunged over the embankment.

There was nothing the driver could do. In a matter of seconds the car rolled and tumbled its way down the steep embankment, finally coming to a rest on its rooftop.

Ivan was upside down in the car and dazed from the trauma of the accident, but he slowly turned himself right side up. The roof of the car had caved in, and all the windows had been shattered. The seats had broken off and were smashed up against the ceiling of the car, and the doors were jammed—there was no way for Ivan or the pastor to get out.

Ivan checked himself over—fortunately, he had suffered nothing more than a few scratches. But was Pastor Stefan all right? Was he still inside the car? Was he unconscious? Was he dead?

"Are you OK, Pastor?" Ivan was afraid to listen for fear that he would hear only silence. But then he heard a moan and, to his relief, the pastor's trembling voice. "I'm OK, Ivan. I'm hurt, but I think I'll be all right."

"Do you have any broken bones?"

"I don't think so. I'm bleeding from the head, but I don't think it's too serious."

"Slava Boeg!" Ivan shouted with joy. "Praise God! See if you can put some pressure on the bleeding—I'm going to try to get us out of here as fast as I can."

Ivan reached for one of the door handles and tried to push the door open, but it wouldn't budge. He tried the other door, but had no luck with it, either—both doors were jammed shut. What should he do? Who would come to their rescue? This was a very lonely road—they hadn't seen another car all day and probably wouldn't.

In desperation Ivan began kicking both of the doors, deliberately at first, and then more frantically. What if there was a gas leak somewhere in the car? What if the car caught on fire? A wave of panic surged through him, and he kicked all the harder.

And then suddenly Ivan came to his senses. God had always been his help and strength—in good times and bad.

"Please, Lord," he prayed, "show me what You want me to do. We need to get out of this car, and right now! You're the only one who can help us do it."

Hardly had he finished his prayer when he heard a voice far away calling faintly but distinctly. "Hello, there! Are you all right! Does anyone need help in there!"

"Over here!" Ivan shouted anxiously, fearing that the person might somehow pass them by. "We're over here!"

When he heard footsteps approaching, he breathed a sigh of relief at the thought that his prayer had been answered! Help had arrived, and so quickly! It was uncanny!

The man reached his hand through a small opening in the crushed metal of the rooftop. "Are you boys all right?" he asked. "Is anyone hurt in there?"

"We're OK," Ivan ventured as he took the man's hand. "My friend in the front seat is bleeding a little, but I think we'll be fine if we can just get out."

As Ivan peered out through the opening, he caught a glimpse of the man's face, and his heart sank. The man was older—maybe 75 or 80 years of age. What could he do? He could go for help, but of course that would take longer.

"Thank you for coming to help us," Ivan said halfheartedly. "It was kind of you. Now, can you figure a way to get us out? I've tried to open the doors back here, but I can't seem to get them to budge. They're jammed for sure."

Ivan heard the old man shuffling around outside, and then suddenly daylight streamed into the cramped space where Ivan lay trapped. The old man had somehow managed to get the door open. He helped Ivan out and checked him for injuries.

"Don't worry about me," Ivan insisted. "I'll be all right!" He noticed that the man was wearing a white shirt and a tie—and he had a short haircut. *Funny how you notice things like that at a time like this*, Ivan mused.

He turned to the car again. "Pastor, are you OK?"

"I'm all right," Pastor Stefan responded, but Ivan could tell by the tone of his voice that he was worried.

"Are you still bleeding?"

"Yes—not a lot, but some."

"We're going to get you out now," Ivan called excitedly. He grabbed the front door handle on the passenger side and gave it a yank. Nothing happened. Ivan tried again, but the door wouldn't budge.

Ivan sank back exhausted on the ground as the old man stepped forward to give the door a try himself. As he took hold of the door, Ivan noticed how powerful his forearms looked—not huge, but sinewy and very strong. It was obvious the man had used them all his life for hard work.

With a sudden jerk the old man pulled the front door open too. Ivan sat gaping in surprise. How had an 80-year-old gentleman managed to open both car doors like that? Ivan was so astonished that he forgot to help the old man pull Pastor Stefan from the car.

The old gentleman sat Pastor Stefan down and helped him stop the bleeding by pressing on the wound with a piece of cloth. "I'm sorry you ruined your nice car," the old man said.

For several moments Pastor Stefan and Ivan just sat on the ground trying to take in everything that had happened. After a bit Ivan stood to his feet to thank the old man, but he was nowhere in sight.

Ivan walked around to the other side of the car, but he wasn't there, either. He scrambled up the embankment and looked up and down the road. Nothing. Ivan turned and looked out across a large pasture in the valley to the south. There were no trees in sight anywhere—just wide-open spaces. Where could the old man have gone so quickly? He had simply disappeared.

Ivan picked his way back down the embankment and sat down beside Pastor Stefan.

"That old man was certainly an answer to our prayers," Pastor Stefan said reverently. "Did you get his name?"

"He's gone," Ivan said.

"Which way did he go?" Pastor Stefan pulled the cloth away from his head to check the bleeding. "We never even got a chance to thank him properly."

"I don't know where he went," Ivan stammered. "He just—disappeared! It was as if he vanished into thin air."

The two of them stared at each other for a long moment.

"Maybe he did," Pastor Stefan replied softly. "Maybe he did."

Ivan and Pastor Stefan discussed the incident time and again in the days that followed, and always they agreed that the old man was probably one of their guardian angels. The question was, whose?

CHAPTER 27

The years came and went. Vera gave birth to two little daughters—and what a blessing they were! After all the years of sacrifice and hardship, sweet little Larisa and Ludmilla were like little angels sent straight from heaven. To Ivan they seemed as delicate as the wild woodland violets, and even prettier.

Vera continued to assist Ivan in his work, traveling with him as often as possible and helping build up the missionary work wherever they went. She was his best and dearest companion, always sharing his burdens, kissing away the threat of fatigue, and soothing the pain of disappointment. It was largely because of her encouragement that Ivan added yet another component to his ministry.

There was a great need to publish Bibles and inspirational books in the Ukrainian and Moldovan languages—such books as *The Great Controversy, The Ministry of Healing,* and *The Desire of Ages.* These and other good books were hard to find and as precious as gold to the members of God's church. And these books would do a world of good if they were taken by Ivan's missionary Bible workers into the army.

But since the books were religious, Ivan couldn't take them to any of the local printing presses to have them published. Even if he could have found enough money to pay for such projects, it would have been illegal to print the books.

The solution came in a group of women from Ivan's local churches who volunteered their time to help duplicate the books. Using old manual typewriters, they spent endless hours typing numerous copies of the books. Of course, this was all done without pay, but to the godly women it was well worth it. If placed in the right hands, the books would prove invaluable.

As usual, their activities were sensitive, because no one knew for sure if there might be KGB informants infiltrating their ranks. And it was always possible that an overzealous "patriotic" neighbor might turn them in. As a result Ivan, Vera, and the volunteers had to work under the greatest secrecy to avoid being discovered, which would result in the confiscation of their books and typewriters.

In spite of all that Satan could throw at Ivan and his coworkers, the missionary work continued to flourish. Ivan was keenly aware that the forces of darkness were working overtime to impede and obstruct his work for God, but the obstacles only made him all the more determined to succeed. In fact, his missionary endeavors became an icon of the church's potential in the Soviet Union. It was a phenomenon never before seen in the history of evangelism in the Russian Republic.

So successful were Ivan's methods in training boys for missionary service in the army—and his efforts to place freshly typed books in their hands—that he was finally hired by the church to begin a full-scale program doing just that. Military-age boys were now systematically trained in every place there was a church that could support them. They were taught the Bible and how to present it in a way that was genuine yet appealing. They were taught to depend on prayer and fasting as their main source of strength in times of need. And they were given the typed copies of Bibles and other good books to take with them when they entered the army.

Over the course of time some 300 young men were trained in this way, each one of exceptional quality. All of them eventually became officers in the military because of their leadership qualities and strength of character. Most became sergeants, but some rose to the level of lieutenant, and even captain.

These men were not afraid to be God's witnesses in one of the mightiest military machines ever to march on the face of the earth. They stepped out in faith during a time that the Word of God was suppressed and everywhere men's hearts failed them for want of hope.

After the fall of the iron curtain in the late 1980s and early 1990s, the Soviet Union splintered and broke into pieces. The prediction in the book of Daniel again proved true, that no nation in the modern era would ever rise up to rule the world—not even the mighty U.S.S.R.

This is a testimony to God's people everywhere, to those who wish to dig deep into the Word of God. It is a witness to those who will listen to the voice of His servants. It is a demonstration of His power in the life and labor of His missionaries clear down to the end of time.

EPILOGUE

For more than 40 years Ivan labored undercover to train young men to enter the army as Bible workers. And with them he sent Bibles and other religious books.

When these young men finished their tour of duty in the military, many returned to their churches to become pastors. In fact, Ivan's system of training was so successful that it was eventually said that some 80 percent of the pastors in the country of Moldova and half of the pastors in the Ukraine were trained by him.

Today many of Ivan's "missionary men" are well-known, high-ranking leaders of the Seventh-day Adventist Church. Some of these leaders include Victor Krushenitsky, who became the ministerial director at the division office in Moscow, Russia. G. V. Kochmar became president of the Moldova Union, and Fyodor Zamostyan became a dynamic worker for God, carrying on the work of Ivan Gumenyuk by training pastors himself. As in their early years, the spiritual example of these men is still sought today because they dared to stand for God.

As I finished the interview with Ivan for this book, I prayerfully asked him whether he could ever really retire—if he could ever actually lay down the mantle God had entrusted to him.

He looked at me with his clear blue eyes and smiled the same boyish grin he must have flashed as a lad. "How can I retire?" he replied. "My love for the young people of this church is what inspires me to fight one more day for God. While I still have the strength I will always be a missionary man for Him. Until Jesus comes again, I will work tirelessly to win, if possible, even one more soul for Him." He paused and, with glistening eyes and a catch in his throat, added, "I don't know if God will ever ask me to stand alone for Him again the way I did during those years in the Russian army, but if He does, I will be ready to do it gladly all over again."

And you know, as I looked into Ivan's earnest face, I believed that even at his age, he would.